Focus on GRAMMAR 1

WORKBOOK

THIRD EDITION

Samuela Eckstut-Didier

ALWAYS LEARNING

PEARSON

**Focus on Grammar 1: An Integrated Skills Approach, Third Edition
Workbook**

Pearson Education, Inc., 10 Bank Street, White Plains, NY 10606

Staff credits: The people who made up the *Focus on Grammar 1, Third Edition,
Workbook* team, representing editorial, production, design, and manufacturing, are:
Aerin Csigay, Christine Edmonds, Nancy Flaggman, Ann France, Lise Minovitz,
Robert Ruvo, and Marian Wassner.

Cover image: Shutterstock.com
Text composition: ElectraGraphics, Inc.
Text font: New Aster

Photo credits: **Page 7** (all) Shutterstock.com; **p. 8** (7) Shutterstock.com, (8)
Shutterstock.com, (9) Dreamstime.com; **p. 17** (middle) age fotostock/George White,
(bottom) Douglas Peebles/Corbis; **p. 71** Mike Blake/Reuters/Corbis; **p. 108** (top left)
ThinkStock LLC/Index Stock Imagery, (top right) Rebecca Cook/Reuters/Corbis,
(bottom left) Stockdisc/Getty Images, (bottom right) Rubberball/Getty Images;
p. 109 (top left) travis manley/Fotolia, (top right) Casa Productions/Corbis, (bottom
left) Shutterstock.com, (bottom right) Shutterstock.com; **p. 124** (middle) Warner
Bros. Pictures/Photofest, (bottom) AF archive/Alamy; **p. 135** (a–c, e, f, h–j)
Shutterstock.com; **p. 146** Shutterstock.com; **p. 147** Shutterstock.com.

Illustrations: **Steve Attoe:** pp. 1, 2, 3 (a–d, f, h), 6–7, 11, 17 (top), 22, 35, 36 (top),
38–39, 41, 46, 48 (1–2), 49 (3–4, 6), 50, 52, 57, 59, 64, 69, 73, 79, 81, 84, 87, 90–91,
92, 95, 96, 100–101, 106–107, 112, 124, 129–130, 131, 134, 140, 148, 157, 162, 168,
169, 174, 177; **Ron Chironna:** p. 28; **ElectraGraphics:** pp. 42, 66, 98, 114 (1–4), 115
(5–8); **Paul McCusker:** p. 143; **Andy Meyer:** pp. 19, 24, 152; **Dusan Petricic:**
pp. 23, 36 (a–g), 170; **Steve Shulman:** pp. 3 (e, g), 13, 18 (a), 55, 70, 76, 77, 108 (3),
109 (bottom), 171–172; **Tom Sperling:** pp. 12, 74, 102; **Gary Torrisi:** pp. 18 (b–h),
30, 31, 47, 48 (5–8), 49 (5), 113, 114 (5–8)

ISBN 10: 0-13-248413-7
ISBN 13: 978-0-13-248413-8

Printed in the United States of America

6 7 8 9 10   16

CONTENTS

D0573125

ABOUT THE AUTHOR

Samuela Eckstut-Didier has taught ESL and EFL for over twenty-five years in the United States, Greece, Italy, and England. Currently she is teaching at Boston University, Center for English Language and Orientation Programs (CELOP). She has authored or co-authored numerous texts for the teaching of English, notably *Center Stage 2, 3,* and *4; Strategic Reading 1, 2,* and *3; What's in a Word? Reading and Vocabulary Building; In the Real World; First Impressions; Beneath the Surface; Widely Read;* and *Finishing Touches.*

UNIT 1

This is / These are; Subject Pronouns

EXERCISE 1: Text Completion

Complete the reading. Use the words from the box. Don't look at your Student Book.

are	husband	is	These	They're	This is
family	~~I'm~~	It's	These are	This	We're

Hi. ____*I'm*____ Steve
      1.
Beck. _____ is
      2.
my apartment in Seattle.

_____ small but
   3.
comfortable.

These _____ my
      4.
CDs. _____ classical
     5.
and jazz. _____ my
     6.
guitar.

_____ my
    7.
pets, Pam and Kip.
They're wonderful. Pam

_____ eight years
    8.
old and can talk. Kip is two

years old.

We like our apartment. _____
       9.
happy here.

I have a great _____.
       10.
_____ are my parents on the left.
   11.
This is my sister Jessica in the middle, with

her _____ and children.
   12.

1

EXERCISE 2: Vocabulary

Look at the people in Steve's family. Who are they? Use the words from the box.

brother	father	mother	son
daughter	husband	sister	wife

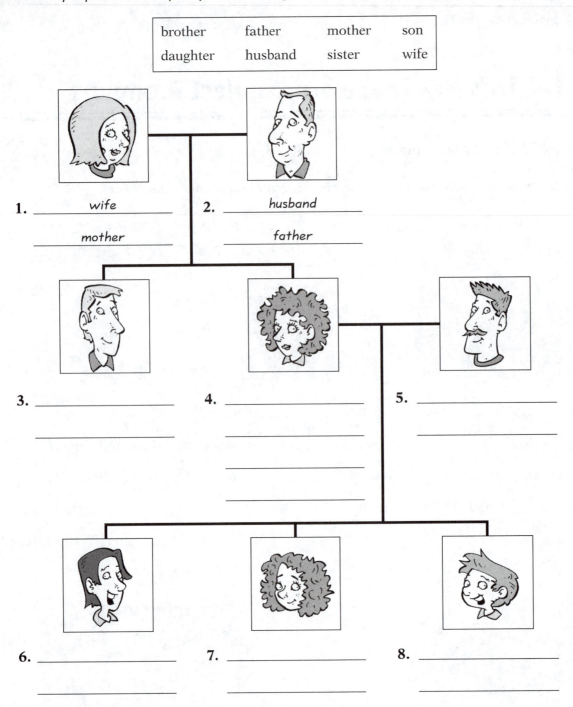

1. _____wife_____   2. _____husband_____

_____mother_____   _____father_____

3. _____   4. _____   5. _____

6. _____   7. _____   8. _____

EXERCISE 3: Subject Pronouns

Complete the sentences with **I, he, she, it, we,** *or* **they.**

Marie-Claire is my friend. _____*She*_____ is from Quebec. Quebec is a city in Canada.
                              1.

_____ is a nice city. Marie-Claire says, "_____ love Quebec. _____
       2.   **3.**   **4.**

is my home." _____ lives in Quebec with her husband, Eric. _____ is
                    5.   **6.**

from New York. _____ are teachers. The school is near their home. _____
                       7.   **8.**

is a big school. Eric says, "_____ are new teachers. Our students are new too.
                                    9.

_____ are very nice."
       10.

EXERCISE 4: *This is / These are*

Look at the pictures. Match the sentences with the pictures.

a.   b.    c.    d.

e.    f.    g.    h.

__*e*__ **1.** This is a ticket.

_____ **2.** These are Jessica's children.

_____ **3.** This is my guitar.

_____ **4.** This is a book.

_____ **5.** These are my pets.

_____ **6.** These are my friends.

_____ **7.** These are my parents.

_____ **8.** This is my friend Pedro.

EXERCISE 5: *This* and *These*: Questions and Statements

Put the words in the correct order. Write sentences. Remember to add the correct capitalization.

1. book / this / your / is / ? <u>Is this your book?</u>

2. pencil / this / your / is / . _____

3. your / is / ticket / this / ? _____

4. keys / are / these / your / . _____

5. my / is / house / this / . _____

6. is / apartment / your / this / ? _____

7. your / these / friends / are / ? _____

8. these / seats / your / are / . _____

EXERCISE 6: *This is* / *These are*

Complete the sentences. Circle the correct answers and write them on the lines.

1. These are my _____<u>parents</u>_____.
   a. parent **(b.)** parents

2. This is my _____.
   a. brother **b.** brothers

3. These are my _____.
   a. sister **b.** sisters

4. These are my _____.
   a. friend **b.** friends

5. This is my _____.
   a. partner **b.** partners

6. This is my _____.
   a. class **b.** classes

EXERCISE 7: Editing

Correct the conversations. There are six mistakes. The first mistake is already corrected.
Find and correct five more.

        this
1. **A:** Is ~~these~~ your ticket?

   B: Yes, it is.

2. **A:** These are your keys?

   B: Yes. Thank you.

3. **A:** This is my car.

   B: She is big.

4. **A:** This are *my* books.

   B: Oh. Sorry.

5. **A:** These are my pet.

   B: They're nice.

6. **A:** Is this your sister?

   B: Yes, her name is Mary. He is a teacher.

EXERCISE 8: Personal Writing

Write sentences about your friends and family.

   EXAMPLE: My sister is eighteen years old.

1. _____

2. _____

3. _____

4. _____

EXERCISE 1: Text Completion

Complete the conversation. Use the words from the box. Don't look at your Student Book.

a	are	Is	these	this	~~What~~
an	I'm	teacher	They're	toaster	what's

ELENA: Judy, _____*what's*_____ this called in
                    1.

English?

JUDY: It's _____ toaster.
                         2.

ELENA: A _____? T-O-A-S-T-E-R?
                    3.

JUDY: That's right.

ELENA: And this?

JUDY: It's _____ oven. O-V-E-N.
                       4.

ELENA: And what's _____ called?
                              5.

JUDY: It's a spoon. S-P-O-O-N.

ELENA: Spoon.

ELENA: _____ this a knife?
                   6.

JUDY: Yes. These _____ knives, and
                           7.

_____ are forks. Knives—
8.

K-N-I-V-E-S. Forks—F-O-R-K-S.

ELENA: Knives, forks.

JUDY: Yes.

Elena: _____ are these?

9.

Judy: _____ glasses. G-L-A-S-S-E-S.

10.

Elena: Thank you. You're a good _____.

11.

Let's go out.

Judy: Not so fast. Now in Portuguese.

This time _____ a student, and

12.

you're a teacher.

EXERCISE 2: Vocabulary

Unscramble the letters to make words. Then add **a** or **an**.

1.

nosop

_a_ _____ _spoon_ _____

2.

geg

_____ _____

3.

nefik

_____ _____

4.

slags

_____ _____

5.

nufmif

_____ _____

6.

geg... pelap

_____ _____

(continued on next page)

7.

8.

9.

garforreteri

nove

voest

____ _____

____ _____

____ _____

EXERCISE 3: Singular and Plural Nouns

A. *Write the sentences in the singular.*

1. These umbrellas are from France. *This umbrella is from France.* _____

2. These apples are from Canada. _____

3. These children are from Haiti. _____

4. The muffins are on the counter. _____

5. The glasses are in the kitchen. _____

B. *Write the sentences in the plural.*

1. This pineapple is from Brazil. *These pineapples are from Brazil.* _____

2. This person is from Mexico. _____

3. This girl is from Japan. _____

4. This knife is from Austria. _____

5. This teacher is from China. _____

EXERCISE 4: Singular and Plural Nouns

Complete the sentences with the singular or plural form of the noun.

1. I have one pet, not two _____pets_____.

2. I have four glasses, not one _____.

3. I have two brothers, not one _____.

4. We have one child, not two _____.

5. I have one good friend, not ten good _____.

6. I have two knives, not one _____.

7. We have one English class, not two English _____.

8. We have one dish, not three _____.

EXERCISE 5: *A* and *An*; Proper Nouns

*Write conversations. Add **a** or **an** where necessary. Circle the proper nouns.*

1. **A:** Is / this / oven / ?   *Is this an oven?*

   B: It's / toaster / .   No. *It's a toaster.*

2. **A:** Are / these / pineapples / from / California / ?   *Are these pineapples from (California?)*

   B: They're / from / Hawaii / .   No. _____

3. **A:** This / is / oven / .   _____

   B: It's / stove / .   No, it isn't. _____

4. **A:** Is / this / apple / ?   _____

   B: It's / apple / .   Yes. _____

5. **A:** Is / Judy / from / Canada / ?   _____

   B: She's / from / England / .   No. _____

6. **A:** Is / Mr. Lopez / student / ?   _____

   B: He's / teacher / .   No. _____

EXERCISE 6: Editing

Correct the conversations. There are eight mistakes. The first mistake is already corrected. Find and correct seven more.

                                     notebooks

1. **A:** Are these your ~~notebook~~?

   B: Yes, they are.

2. **A:** Is Jessica from a China?

   B: Yes. She's student in my class.

3. **A:** These are a forks.

   B: No, they aren't. They're spoons. This is fork.

4. **A:** This refrigerators is big.

   B: Yes, it is.

5. **A:** These is my kitchen.

   B: It's big!

6. **A:** What's this?

   B: It's a orange.

EXERCISE 7: Personal Writing

Write sentences about things in your pocket, your wallet, or your bag.

    EXAMPLE: *These are my keys.*

1. _____

2. _____

3. _____

4. _____

UNIT
3 Present of *Be*: Statements

EXERCISE 1: Text Completion

Complete the conversation. Use the words from the box. Don't look at your Student Book.

am	from	not
Australia	I	They're
clean	is	~~This~~
delicious	It's	you

MARK: Hi, Steve.

STEVE: Hi, Mark. Uh, Mark. _____*This*_____ is my cousin Amy, and this

　　　　　　　1.

_____ her friend Jenny. _____ here on vacation.
　　2.　　　　　　　　　　　　　　　3.

MARK: Hi. Nice to meet you.

AMY: Nice to meet you too.

MARK: So you're _____ from around here?
　　　　　　　　　4.

AMY: No. We're from _____.
　　　　　　　　　　　　5.

MARK: Australia? That's pretty far away. Are you from Melbourne?

AMY: No. We're from Sydney. How about _____? Are you
　　　　　　　　　　　　　　　　　　　　　　　6.

_____ Seattle?
　　7.

MARK: Yes, I _____.
　　　　　　　　8.

AMY: Jenny and I love Seattle. It's a beautiful and _____ city. The people
　　　　　　　　　　　　　　　　　　　　　　　　　　9.

are friendly. And the coffee is _____.
　　　　　　　　　　　　　　　10.

MARK: How's Sydney?

AMY: _____ a great city too—and not just because _____
　　　　11.　　　　　　　　　　　　　　　　　　　　　　　　　12.

live there!

Circle the correct words to make true statements.

1. The people **are /** **aren't** friendly.

   They **are** / **aren't** unfriendly.

2. The street **is / isn't** dirty.

   It **'s / isn't** clean.

3. The restaurant **is / isn't** popular.

   It **'s / isn't** unpopular.

4. I **'m / 'm not** at a great party.

   I **'m / 'm not** at a terrible party.

5. The coffee **is / isn't** delicious.

   It **'s / isn't** awful.

6. They **'re / 're not** expensive.

   They **'re / 're not** reasonable.

EXERCISE 3: *Be*: Affirmative and Negative Statements

Look at the pictures. Put a check (✓) next to the true statements.

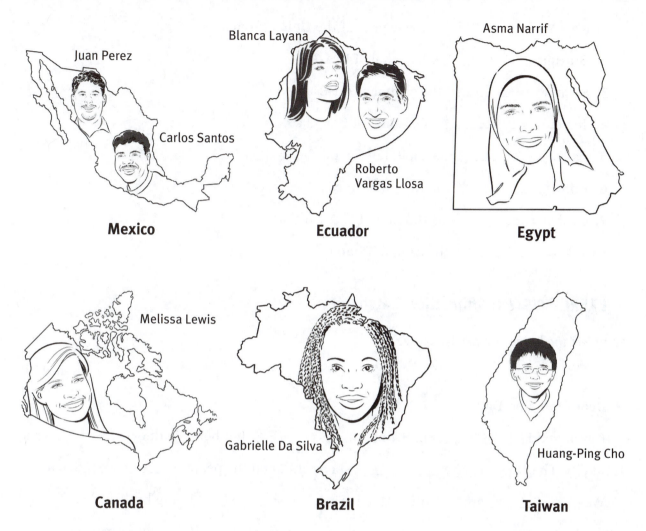

Mexico — Juan Perez, Carlos Santos

Ecuador — Blanca Layana, Roberto Vargas Llosa

Egypt — Asma Narrif

Canada — Melissa Lewis

Brazil — Gabrielle Da Silva

Taiwan — Huang-Ping Cho

_____ **1.** I'm Huang-Ping Cho. I'm from Egypt.

✓ **2.** This is Gabrielle Da Silva. She's from Brazil.

_____ **3.** I'm Roberto Vargas Llosa. I'm not from Mexico.

_____ **4.** They are Juan Perez and Carlos Santos. They're from Peru.

_____ **5.** I'm Huang-Ping Cho. I'm not from Japan.

_____ **6.** This is Melissa Lewis. She's from Australia.

_____ **7.** They are Blanca Layana and Roberto Vargas Llosa. They aren't from Brazil.

_____ **8.** This is Asma Narrif. She's from Egypt.

EXERCISE 4: *Be*: Affirmative and Negative Statements

Complete the sentences. Use **is** *or* **isn't**.

1. New York ____isn't____ the capital of the United States.

2. Brasília ____is____ the capital of Brazil.

3. Sydney _____ the capital of Australia.

4. Toronto _____ the capital of Canada.

5. Cairo _____ the capital of Egypt.

6. Rome _____ the capital of Italy.

7. Canberra _____ the capital of Australia.

8. Tokyo _____ the capital of Japan.

EXERCISE 5: *Be*: Affirmative Statements

Complete the letter. Use **am, is,** *or* **are**.

January 21

Dear Mom and Dad,

Karen and I ____are____ in Sydney. It _____ hot here. Sydney _____ a
    1.   2.   3.

great city. The Opera House _____ beautiful, and the people _____ friendly.
            4.   5.

We _____ at the Garden Hotel. The rooms _____ big but a little
    6.   7.

expensive. Karen _____ in the hotel room now. I _____ at a very nice
        8.   9.

restaurant. The food _____ delicious.
         10.

Love,

Paul

EXERCISE 6: *Be*: Contractions of Affirmative and Negative Statements

Rewrite the sentences with the full forms of the contractions.

1. I'm from Ecuador. _I am from Ecuador._

2. It's terrible there. _____

3. She's not popular. _____

4. We're not here on business. _____

5. You're friendly. _____

6. They aren't from Seattle. _____

EXERCISE 7: *Be*: Contractions of Affirmative and Negative Statements

Rewrite the sentences with contractions.

1. It is not dirty. _It's not dirty._ OR _It isn't dirty._ _____

2. We are from Tokyo. _____

3. They are not here. _____

4. I am not the teacher. _____

5. He is my cousin. _____

6. You are from here. _____

EXERCISE 8: Editing

Correct these conversations. There are ten mistakes. The first two mistakes are already corrected. Find and correct eight more.

1. **A:** ~~Are~~ *Is* Mark from around here?

   B: Yes, ~~they~~ *he* is.

2. **A:** The food good?

   B: Is terrible.

3. **A:** This my cousin.

   B: Are she a student?

4. **A:** Be you from Mexico?

   B: No, we're are from Peru.

5. **A:** Your cousins Amy and Mary are here on vacation?

   B: No, they here on business.

EXERCISE 9: Personal Writing

Write sentences about a city in your country, but not your city.

EXAMPLE: *San Francisco is a popular city.*

1. _____

2. _____

3. _____

4. _____

That is / Those are; Possessive Adjectives

EXERCISE 1: Text Completion

Complete the conversations. Use the words from the box. Don't look at your Student Book.

Are	building	How about	It's	stadiums	those
a great idea	her	isn't	its	~~That's~~	your

STEVE: Well, here we are. _____That's_____ the Space
                    1.

Needle. _____ a picture?
          2.

AMY: Sure. Too bad Jenny _____ here, but I
              3.

have _____ camera.
      4.

STEVE: Come on. Let's go up.

*****

AMY: Wow! Look at _____ buildings.
          5.

STEVE: They're the _____. Here, take a look.
          6.

AMY: They're big! _____ those people next to
          7.

them? They look so small.

STEVE: Yep. Now look over there. That's the University of Washington.

AMY: That's _____ university, right?
          8.

STEVE: Yes. OK, now look down. Look at that colored

_____.
          9.

AMY: The colors are beautiful, but _____
                           10.

shape is really unusual.

STEVE: That's the EMP. _____ a music
             11.

museum. It belongs to Paul Allen. It's his "baby."

AMY: Let's go see it.

STEVE: That's _____.
          12.

EXERCISE 2: Vocabulary

Look at the pictures. Match the sentences with the pictures.

a.
b.
c.
d.

e.
f.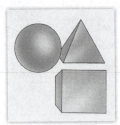
g.
h.

___c___ **1.** That's a stadium.

_____ **2.** That's a beautiful concert hall.

_____ **3.** That's our park.

_____ **4.** Those are coffee shops.

_____ **5.** Those are tall buildings.

_____ **6.** That's a movie theater.

_____ **7.** That's a camera.

_____ **8.** Those are shapes.

EXERCISE 3: *This, That, These,* and *Those*

Read the conversations. Circle the correct words to complete them.

1. **A:** What's **this /** ⟨**that**⟩ over there?

   B: **This / That**? The Space Needle.

2. **A:** Wow! What are **these / those** big buildings over there?

   B: **These / Those** are the stadiums.

3. **A:** Excuse me. Is **this / these** your seat?

   B: Yes, it is. Sorry. But **those / that** seat over there is free.

4. **A:** **These / This** is a very nice photo. Are **this / these** your children?

   B: Yes, they are. **These / That** are my sons, Juan and Pedro.

5. **A:** Mark, **this / that** is my friend Jenny. She's from Sydney.

   B: Hi, Jenny. Is **this / that** your first vacation in Seattle?

Complete the story. Use **my, his, her, our,** *or* **their.**

That's me and _____*my*_____ family. Those are _____ sisters. _____
              1.   **2.**   **3.**

names are Kate, Ann, and Ruth. And that's _____ little brother. _____ name
                                            4.   **5.**

is Sam. _____ parents aren't in the picture. Kate and _____ husband have
               6.   **7.**

one daughter. _____ name is Amy.
                    8.

EXERCISE 5: Subject Pronouns and Possessive Adjectives

Complete the conversations. Circle the correct answers. Write the words on the lines.

1. **A:** My name's Serena.

   B: _____*It's*_____ a beautiful name.

   a. Its   (**b.**) It's

2. **A:** _____ wrong.

   a. Your   **b.** You're

   B: No, I'm not.

3. **A:** Steve and Amy aren't here.

   B: But _____ car is here.

   a. their   **b.** they're

4. **A:** _____ camera is nice.

   a. Your   **b.** You're

   B: Thanks.

5. **A:** Are those your pets?

   B: No, _____ my brother's pets.

   a. their   **b.** they're

6. **A:** Is that your cat?

   B: Yes, _____ name is Ernie.

   a. its   **b.** it's

EXERCISE 6: Editing

Correct the conversations. There are ten mistakes. The first two mistakes are already corrected. Find and correct eight more.

1. **A:** Is that ~~you're~~ *your* book?

   B: Yes, ~~its~~ *it* is.

2. **A:** Are that your children?

   B: No, their my brother's son and daughter.

3. **A:** Is those your glasses?

   B: No, these my sunglasses.

4. A: That people are teachers.

    B: His names are Steve Beck and Annie Macintosh.

5. A: That is your cousin?

    B: Yes, she name is Jessica.

EXERCISE 7: Personal Writing

Imagine you are showing someone a picture of a famous place in your country's capital city. Write four sentences.

    EXAMPLE: *That's the White House. It's in Washington, D.C. It's the home of the U.S. president and his family. It's very big.*

1. _____

2. _____

3. _____

4. _____

Present of *Be*: *Yes / No* Questions, Questions with *Who* and *What*

Complete the conversations. Use the words from the box. Don't look at your Student Book.

~~Are~~	Her	he is	it	she's	Who's
does	He's	Is	she	What	Yes

STEVE: Mark?

MARK: Steve! _____*Are*_____ you here for the wedding?
 1.

STEVE: _____, I am. Amanda is my cousin. What
 2.
about you?

MARK: Josh and I are friends from school. Boy, this is a great

wedding.

STEVE: Yes, _____ is.
 3.

KATHY: _____ that man with Steve?
 4.

AMANDA: His name is Mark. He and Josh are friends.

KATHY: Hmm. _____ he single?
 5.

AMANDA: Yes, _____.
 6.

KATHY: What _____ he do?
 7.

AMANDA: _____ a student and a writer.
 8.

KATHY: What kind of writer?

AMANDA: He writes travel books.

MARK: Who's that woman with Amanda?

STEVE: _____ name is Kathy.
 9

MARK: Is _____ married?
 10.

STEVE: No, _____ not.
 11.

MARK: Hmm . . . _____ does she do?
12.

STEVE: She's a travel agent.

EXERCISE 2: Vocabulary

Look at the pictures. Circle the correct answers.

1.

Is she a cashier?

a. Yes, she is.

b. No, she isn't.

2.

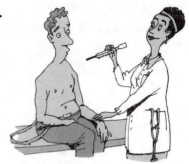

Is she a police officer?

a. Yes, she is

b. No, she isn't.

3.

Is he a mechanic?

a. Yes, he is.

b. No, he isn't.

4.

Is he a nurse?

a. Yes, he is.

b. No, he isn't.

5.

Is he a travel agent?

a. Yes, he is.

b. No, he isn't.

6.

Is he a clerk?

a. Yes, he is.

b. No, he isn't.

Write two conversations. Use the sentences from the box.

Diaz.	Is she a good teacher?
Travel books.	What does she write?
She's a writer.	~~Is that your wife?~~
Yes. Her name's Ellen.	What does she do?
Yes. And she's friendly too.	~~Who's that woman?~~
That's Amy. She's my teacher.	What's her last name?

Conversation 1

A: Who's that woman?

B: _____

A: _____

B: _____

A: _____

B: _____

Conversation 2

A: Is that your wife?

B: _____

A: _____

B: _____

A: _____

B: _____

Write questions to complete the conversations. Put the words in the correct order.

1. A: you / student / a / Are / ?

     Are you a student?

  B: Yes, I am.

2. A: she / Is / sister / your / ?

_____

B: No, she isn't. She's my cousin.

3. A: that / Who / is / woman / ?

_____

B: She's my teacher.

4. A: father / a / your / Is / dentist / ?

_____

B: No, he's not. He's a police officer.

5. A: their / name / is / What / last / ?

_____

B: It's Lee.

6. A: do / friend / does / What / your / ?

_____

B: Steve? Oh, he's a nurse.

EXERCISE 5: Short Answers with the Present of _Be_

Answer the questions. Write true short answers with the correct form of **be.**

1. Are you a student? _Yes, I am._ _____

2. Are you single? _____

3. Are you friendly? _____

4. Is your teacher married? _____

5. Is your teacher from Canada? _____

6. Is your classroom big? _____

7. Are your classmates happy? _____

8. Are you and your classmates friends? _____

EXERCISE 6: Questions with *Who* and *What*

Complete the questions in the chart with **Who** or **What**. Then write short answers.

	Questions	Long Answers	Short Answers
1.	_____What_____'s your name?	It's Mary.	Mary.
2.	_____'s that student?	That's Ben.	
3.	_____ are they?	They're my grandchildren.	
4.	_____'s that?	It's a camera.	

EXERCISE 7: Questions with *Who* and *What*

Complete the questions in the chart with **Who** or **What**. Then write long answers.

	Questions	Short Answers	Long Answers
1.	_____Who_____'s that man?	My brother.	That's my brother.
2.	_____'s his name?	Peter.	
3.	_____'s the capital of Australia?	Canberra.	
4.	_____'s the teacher of this class?	Lynn Martin.	

EXERCISE 8: Editing

Correct the conversations. There are ten mistakes. The first mistake is already corrected. Find and correct nine more.

1. **A:** ~~Who's~~ What's her last name?

   B: Martinez.

2. **A:** You and Joe married?

   B: Yes, we're.

3. **A:** Who be that boy?

   B: That my son.

4. **A:** Who is the capital of the United States?

   B: Is Washington, D.C.

5. **A:** That woman your mother?

   B: Yes, she's.

6. **A:** Bob a clerk is?

   B: No, he isn't.

EXERCISE 9: Personal Writing

Write four questions to ask your teacher.

EXAMPLES: *Are you married?*
Who's your favorite singer?

1. _____

2. _____

3. _____

4. _____

EXERCISE 1: Text Completion

Complete the email messages. Use the words from the box. Don't look at your Student Book.

at	bus	floor	gym	Her	party
between	corner	from	~~Hi~~	is	Where's

Subj: Yuko's birthday
Date: Wednesday, November 3
From: judyjohnson@uw.edu
   To: mm@uw.edu

a birthday cake

_____ *Hi* _____, Mark,
     1.

I want to go to Yuko's _____, but I don't have her address. _____ her
         2.   **3.**

new apartment?

Judy

Subj: Re: Yuko's birthday
Date: Wednesday, November 3
From: mm@uw.edu
   To: judyjohnson@uw.edu

a gift

Hi, Judy,

Her apartment _____ on First Avenue _____ Jackson and Main. (I think
         4.   **5.**

it's _____ 10 First Avenue, but I'm not sure.) It's across _____ a library
   6.   **7.**

and next to a _____. She's on the second _____, Apartment 2A. Take
          8.   **9.**

the number 4 _____. It stops on the _____ of First and Jackson.
           10.   **11.**

(_____ phone number is 206–555–2343.)
   12.

See you Saturday.

Mark

EXERCISE 2: Vocabulary

One word in each group is spelled wrong. Write the word correctly. Don't look at your Student Book.

1. supermarket

   apartement building

   bank

   apartment building

2. movie theater

   park

   hospitol

   _____

3. gym

   resterant

   post office

   _____

4. museam

   supermarket

   restaurant

   _____

5. libary

   gym

   post office

   _____

6. coffee shop

   movie thaeter

   library

   _____

EXERCISE 3: Prepositions of Place

Look at the map. Read the sentences. Write **T (True)** *or* **F (False)**.

___F___ **1.** The movie theater is across from the restaurant.

___T___ **2.** The post office is across from the movie theater.

_____ **3.** The bank is between the post office and the art museum.

_____ **4.** The art museum is between the restaurant and the movie theater.

_____ **5.** The art museum is next to the post office.

_____ **6.** The restaurant is on Washington Street.

_____ **7.** The post office is at number 21 First Avenue.

_____ **8.** The art museum is across from the restaurant.

Read the description and look at the picture. Write the correct place names next to the numbers for the buildings.

The bank is at the corner of Tenth Street and West Avenue. It's next to the post office. The movie theater is at the corner of Ninth Street and East Avenue. The art museum is on Ninth Street next to the movie theater. The park is across from the restaurant and the theater. The apartment building is across from the post office. It's between the supermarket and the library. The supermarket is across from the bank.

1. *bank* _____

2. _____

3. _____

4. _____

5. _____

6. _____

7. _____

8. _____

9. _____

EXERCISE 5: The Present of *Be*: Questions with *Where*

*Write a question for each answer. Use **where** in each question.*

1. **A:** Where's Ana from? OR Where is Ana from?

   B: Ana? She's from Brazil.

2. **A:** _____

   B: Mr. and Mrs. Lin? They're from Australia.

3. **A:** _____

   B: The doctors? They're from Mexico.

4. **A:** _____

   B: Paul? He's from Haiti.

5. **A:** _____

   B: I'm from the United States.

EXERCISE 6: Ordinal Numbers

Complete the chart.

	Number	Word	Ordinal Number	Ordinal Word
1.	4	four	4th	fourth
2.	6	six		
3.	1			first
4.	9	nine		
5.	8		8th	
6.	2			second
7.	3	three		
8.	7		7th	
9.	10			tenth
10.	5		5th	

Look at the sign. Answer the questions. Spell out the ordinal numbers.

MAIN STREET MEDICAL BUILDING	
	Floor
Doctor Bell	5
Doctor Chan	1
Doctor Din	3
Doctor Lugo	4
Doctor Peterson	6
Doctor Shore	2

1. Where's Doctor Bell's office? *It's on the fifth floor.* _____

2. Where's Doctor Chan's office? _____

3. Where's Doctor Din's office? _____

4. Where's Doctor Lugo's office? _____

5. Where's Doctor Peterson's office? _____

6. Where's Doctor Shore's office? _____

EXERCISE 8: Editing

Correct the email messages. There are seven mistakes. The first mistake is already corrected. Find and correct six more.

Subj: Phone number and address
Date: Friday, June 10
From: BobMcDonald@MU.edu
To: PLM@MU.edu

Hi, Paula,

What's your phone number, and ~~what's~~ *where's* your apartment? Is it on Main Street? And what

floor is your apartment in?

Bob

Subj: Re: Phone number and address
Date: Saturday, June 11
From: PLM@MU.edu
To: BobMcDonald@MU.edu

Hi, Bob,

My phone number 555–0900. My apartment isn't at Main Street. It's on 212 Park

Avenue. Take the number 12 bus. My apartment building is next the post office, and

my apartment is on the nine floor.

Paula

EXERCISE 9: Personal Writing

Write an email message about the location of your home. See the email message from Mark on page 48 of your Student Book for an example.

_____

_____

_____

_____

UNIT 7   Past of *Be*: Statements, *Yes / No* Questions

Complete the conversation. Use the words from the box. Don't look at your Student Book.

| funny | it | movies | was | Were | Were you |
| I wasn't | last | ~~This~~ | wasn't | weren't | you |

KATHY: Hello?

AMANDA: Hi, Kathy. _____*This*_____ is Amanda.
1.

KATHY: Hi, Amanda. How's it going?

AMANDA: Fine. Hey, Josh and I stopped by your house _____ night, but you
2.

_____ there. Or were _____ asleep? I guess we were
3.   4.

there about 9:00.

KATHY: Actually, I _____ at home last night. I was at the _____.
5.   6.

AMANDA: _____ you with Olivia?
7.

KATHY: No, _____.
8.

AMANDA: With Sally?

KATHY: No.

(continued on next page)

AMANDA: _____ alone?
9.

KATHY: Uh, no. I was with . . . someone. The movie

_____ great. Really exciting. And
10.

_____ too.
11.

AMANDA: Really! What movie was _____?
12.

KATHY: *Frankenstein's Uncle.*

EXERCISE 2: Vocabulary

Look at the pictures. Match the sentences with the pictures.

a.

b.

c.

d.

e.

f.

g.

___e___ **1.** The movie was exciting.   _____ **5.** The television show was boring.

_____ **2.** The television show was funny.   _____ **6.** The man was asleep at the movies.

_____ **3.** The man was alone at the movies.   _____ **7.** The television show was scary.

_____ **4.** The movie was interesting.

EXERCISE 3: Past of *Be*: Affirmative and Negative Statements

Read the sentences. Write **T (True)** *or* **F (False)**.

_____ **1.** I was late for class yesterday.

_____ **2.** I wasn't at the library last night.

_____ **3.** A friend was with me yesterday.

_____ **4.** My teacher wasn't at school yesterday.

_____ **5.** My friends and I were at a movie yesterday.

_____ **6.** My family and I were at home last night.

_____ **7.** My friends were at my home last night.

_____ **8.** My classmates weren't at the game yesterday.

EXERCISE 4: Past of *Be*: Affirmative and Negative Statements

Complete the sentences. Use **was, wasn't, were,** *or* **weren't** *and* **yesterday**.

1. Jack's at home today, but _he wasn't at home yesterday._

2. Jenny wasn't in class today, but _she was in class yesterday._

3. I'm happy today, but _____

4. It's cold today, but _____

5. The children are not at a soccer game today, but _____

6. We aren't tired today, but _____

7. The streets aren't dirty today, but _____

8. You're at the library today, but _____

9. I'm not home today, but _____

10. The boys are at the movies today, but _____

EXERCISE 5: Past of *Be*: Affirmative and Negative Statements

Complete Kathy's diary. Use **was, wasn't, were,** *or* **weren't.**

April 15

    Yesterday _____*was*_____ great. I _____ alone. I _____ with
           1.   **2.**   **3.**

Mark. We _____ at a movie. The movie _____ *Frankenstein's Uncle*. It
             4.   **5.**

_____ really funny.
   6.

    Amanda and Josh _____ with Mark and me. They stopped by my house, but
                         7.

I _____ home. Amanda doesn't know Mark and I _____ together.
  8.   **9.**

EXERCISE 6: Past of *Be*: Yes / No Questions and Short Answers

Look at the pictures. Write questions. Use the words in parentheses and the correct form of **be.** *Then write short answers and give more information.*

1. (Bill and Steve / at a movie / last night)

   Were Bill and Steve at a movie last night?   _No, they weren't. They were at a concert._

2. (Jeremy / at a soccer game / yesterday)

   _____   _Yes, he was. It was exciting._

3. (Tim and Jessica / at a play / yesterday)

_____   _____

4. (Judy / at a party / last night)

_____   _____

5. (Mark / at a soccer game / yesterday)

_____   _____

6. (Amy, Steve, and Jenny / at a party / last night)

_____   _____

EXERCISE 7: Editing

Correct the conversations. There are seven mistakes. The first mistake is already corrected. Find and correct six more.

1. **A:** ~~They were~~ at home yesterday?
   Were they

   B: Yes, they was.

2. **A:** Hi. How it going?

   B: Great.

3. **A:** Were the movie funny yesterday?

   B: No, it isn't.

4. **A:** Where were you the last night?

   B: Was at home.

EXERCISE 8: Personal Writing

Write four sentences about a TV program.

EXAMPLE: American Idol was on TV last night. The program was great. Two singers were really good. One singer wasn't very good.

1. _____

2. _____

3. _____

4. _____

Past of *Be*: *Wh-* Questions

EXERCISE 1: Text Completion

Complete the conversation. Use the words from the box. Don't look at your Student Book.

cool	guide	long	vacation	was	Who
food	~~How~~	tour	weather	were	you

JASON: Hi, Mark.

MARK: Hey, Jason.

JASON: Welcome back. _____*How*_____ was
_____**1.**

your vacation?

MARK: Great.

JASON: You look good. Where were

_____?
2.

MARK: In Spain.

JASON: Nice. How _____ were you there?
3.

MARK: Ten days. Ten wonderful days.

JASON: That's a long _____. My parents _____ there last month.
4. **5.**

It was hot. How was the _____?
6.

MARK: Hot and sunny. But it was _____ at the beach.
7.

JASON: And the _____?
8.

MARK: Delicious.

JASON: So . . . were you on a _____?
9.

MARK: No, but I _____ with a guide.
10.

JASON: A guide? _____ was your guide?
11.

MARK: Remember Kathy? At Amanda's wedding? The travel agent?

JASON: Sure.

(continued on next page)

Mark: Well, she's in Barcelona this month. She was my _____.

12.

Jason: You lucky man!

EXERCISE 2: Vocabulary

Look at the weather information. Answer the questions.

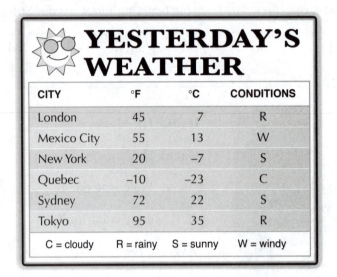

YESTERDAY'S WEATHER

CITY	°F	°C	CONDITIONS
London	45	7	R
Mexico City	55	13	W
New York	20	–7	S
Quebec	–10	–23	C
Sydney	72	22	S
Tokyo	95	35	R

C = cloudy   R = rainy   S = sunny   W = windy

1. How was the weather in London yesterday? *It was cool and rainy.* _____

2. How was the weather in Mexico City yesterday? _____

3. How was the weather in New York yesterday? _____

4. How was the weather in Quebec yesterday? _____

5. How was the weather in Sydney yesterday? _____

6. How was the weather in Tokyo yesterday? _____

EXERCISE 3: *Wh-* Questions with the Past of *Be*

Complete the questions. Use the words from the box. Use some words more than once.

How	How long	When	Where	Who

1. **A:** _____ *How* _____ was the weather yesterday?

   B: It was cool and sunny.

2. **A:** _____ were you in Spain?

   B: Two weeks ago.

3. A: _____ were you last Tuesday?

   B: I was on vacation.

4. A: _____ were you with last weekend?

   B: My parents. They came to visit.

5. A: _____ was your weekend?

   B: It was a lot of fun.

6. A: _____ was the concert?

   B: About two hours.

7. A: _____ was at the museum with you?

   B: Our guide.

EXERCISE 4: Past of *Be: Wh-* Questions and Long Answers

Put the words in the correct order. Write questions. Then write true long answers.

1. Saturday / you / on / were / Where / ?

   Where were you on Saturday?

   I was at the library.

2. class / your / How / was / English / long / ?

   _____

   _____

3. you / at / the / When / supermarket / were / ?

   _____

   _____

4. was / weather / the / How / yesterday / ?

   _____

   _____

5. yesterday / you / Where / were / ?

   _____

   _____

(continued on next page)

6. you / Who / with / last / weekend / were / ?

_____

_____

EXERCISE 5: Past of _Be_: _Wh-_ Questions and Short Answers

Read Jason's postcard. Answer Mark's questions. Use short answers.

                                July 4

Hi, James,

    It's great here in San Francisco.   James O' Malley
I'm here on vacation for five days   111 Washington Ave.
with my brother and sister.   Seattle, WA 98101
The weather isn't great. It's cool and
rainy, but we're having fun. See you
next week.

                                Jason

MARK: James said you went on vacation. When did you go?

JASON: _Last week._____
                    1.

MARK: How was your vacation?

JASON: _____
                    2.

MARK: Where were you?

JASON: _____
                    3.

MARK: Who were you with?

JASON: _____
                    4.

MARK: How long were you there?

JASON: _____
                    5.

MARK: How was the weather?

JASON: _____
                    6.

EXERCISE 6: Editing

Correct the conversations. There are six mistakes. The first mistake is already corrected.
Find and correct five more.

1. A: Where ~~you were~~ *were you* last Saturday?

    B: I was on a tour.

2. A: Who were the students?

    B: They were in the classroom.

3. A: How long class?

    B: Two hours.

4. A: How was the weather?

    B: Was sunny and warm.

5. A: When was they here?

    B: Last Friday.

6. A: How long was the movie?

    B: It was very funny!

EXERCISE 7: Personal Writing

Write four sentences about last weekend.

EXAMPLE: *The weather was beautiful last weekend. It was warm and sunny. I was with my*
family. We were at home.

1. _____

2. _____

3. _____

4. _____

UNIT 9 Imperatives

EXERCISE 1: Text Completion

Complete the conversation. Use the words from the box. Don't look at your Student Book.

corner	go	Indian	Please	right	truck
Don't	Is	park here	~~restaurant~~	sign	Turn

MARK: Is the _____*restaurant*_____ close? I'm hungry.
                1.

STEVE: Yes, it is.

MARK: Is it good?

STEVE: _____ worry. It's very good. It's Indian.
        2.

MARK: Great. I love _____ food.
                  3.

STEVE: Now drive to the _____ and turn left
                        4.

       at Jackson Street.

MARK: At the gas station?

STEVE: Yes. Then _____ two blocks on
                   5.

       Jackson.

MARK: Got it.

STEVE: OK. _____ right at the next corner.
            6.

MARK: At Third Avenue?

STEVE: Yes. The restaurant is on the corner on your

       _____.
         7.

MARK: _____ that it?
         8.

STEVE: Yes, it is. Don't _____. It's a bus stop. Park behind the

9.

_____.

10.

MARK: OK. _____ hand me my jacket . . . Uh, wait a second . . . Steve? The

11.

restaurant is empty.

STEVE: Really? It's usually packed.

MARK: Is that a _____ on the door?

12.

STEVE: Uh-huh . . . Closed for vacation.

EXERCISE 2: Vocabulary

Write the words next to the correct pictures.

a bus stop	a restaurant	~~empty~~	turn left
a gas station	a truck	park	turn right

1. _____empty_____

2. _____

3. _____

4. _____

(continued on next page)

5. _____

6. _____

7. _____

8. _____

EXERCISE 3: Affirmative and Negative Imperatives

Look at the pictures. Circle the correct answers.

1. **a.** Park here.
   b. Don't park here. It's a bus stop.

2. **a.** Sit down.
   b. Don't sit down.

3. a. Close your books.

    b. Don't close your books.

4. a. Don't open the door.

    b. Please open the door.

5. a. Don't turn left. Turn right.

    b. Don't turn right. Turn left.

6. a. Open your eyes.

    b. Don't open your eyes.

EXERCISE 4: Instructions

Write instructions. Use the words from the box.

Answer	Circle	Look at	Read	Write
Ask	Listen to	Open	Underline	

1. _____*Open*_____ the book.

_____*Read*_____

_____*Look at*_____

2. _____ the CD.

_____

(continued on next page)

3. _____ the board.

_____

4. _____ the teacher.

_____

_____

_____

5. _____ the group.

_____

6. _____ the word _English_.

_____

_____

EXERCISE 5: Requests

*Write the requests. Use **please** and the words from the box. Add **don't** where necessary.*

call me	give me a glass of water	open your books
close the windows	~~hand me my jacket~~	~~sit there~~
drive me to school	help me with the bags	

1. I'm cold. _Hand me my jacket, please._

2. That's my seat. _Please don't sit there._

3. This is a test. _____

4. I'm late. _____

5. I'm busy. _____

6. I'm hot. _____

7. I'm thirsty. _____

8. My hands are full. _____

EXERCISE 6: Editing

Correct the conversations. There are six mistakes. The first mistake is already corrected.
Find and correct five more.

      Don't

1. A: ~~No~~ park here. It's a bus stop.

   B: Oh. OK.

2. A: You no go straight at the corner. Turn left.

   B: Got it.

3. A: Please you don't close the window. It's hot!

   B: Sure. No problem.

4. A: Drives one block. Then turn you right.

   B: OK. Thanks.

5. A: Open please the door.

   B: Sure.

EXERCISE 7: Personal Writing

Write directions from a bus stop or subway station to your home.

   EXAMPLE: *At the bus stop turn right. Walk two blocks. Turn right on Master Street. My apartment building is at 463 Master Street. It's on the right. I'm in apartment 2B. Don't use the elevator. Just walk up the stairs. My apartment is on the left.*

_____

_____

_____

_____

EXERCISE 1: Text Completion

Complete the conversation. Use the words from the box. Don't look at your Student Book.

doesn't	is	likes	looks	surfs	watch
have	like	lives	~~need~~	teaches	writes

JUDY: I _____*need*_____ more coffee. Would you like

      1.

some?

MARK: Yes, please.

JUDY: Here you go.

MARK: Thanks.

JUDY: Oh! New photos?

MARK: Yes . . . Look at this one. This _____

           2.

my brother, Nick. He _____ in Kenya.

          3.

He _____ English there.

    4.

JUDY: In Kenya? Wow! . . . He _____ like you.

        5.

MARK: I know. We both _____ brown hair and

      6.

green eyes.

JUDY: And you're both tall.

MARK: But we're different in a lot of ways.

JUDY: How?

MARK: Well, I _____ people and parties.

      7.

Nick _____ computers. Nick

      8.

_____ like parties.

  9.

JUDY: Anything else?

MARK: Uh-huh. I speak Chinese. Nick speaks Swahili.

I read newspapers and magazines. Nick reads

novels. I call my friends. I _____ DVDs almost every night, but Nick
                                      10.

_____ the Internet. He emails me a lot. He _____ a blog
           11.   **12.**

too.

JUDY: Yeah? He sounds interesting.

EXERCISE 2: Vocabulary

A. *Check (✓) the sentences that are true for you.*

_____ **1.** I look like my mother.

_____ **2.** My father often surfs the Internet.

_____ **3.** My grandparents read newspapers and magazines.

_____ **4.** I like novels.

_____ **5.** My brother writes a blog.

B. *Check (✓) the sentences you think are true.*

_____ **1.** 50,000,000 people speak Arabic.

_____ **2.** 10,000,000,000 people speak Chinese.

_____ **3.** 85,000,000 people speak English.

_____ **4.** 250,000,000 people speak French.

_____ **5.** 8,000,000 people speak Italian.

_____ **6.** 14,000,000 people speak Japanese.

_____ **7.** 200,000,000 people speak Korean.

_____ **8.** 1,000,000 people speak Portuguese

_____ **9.** 75,000,000 people speak Spanish.

_____ **10.** 200,000,000 people speak Swahili.

EXERCISE 3: Simple Present Statements: Affirmative and Negative

Complete the sentences. Circle the correct answers. Write the words on the lines.

1. Jessica _____*has*_____ a brother.

  a. have   **b.** having   **c.** has

2. Jessica and Tim _____ three children.

  a. having   **b.** have   **c.** has

3. Steve doesn't _____ children.

  a. have   **b.** has   **c.** having

(continued on next page)

4. Mary _____ with her children, Jessica and Steve.

   a. no lives   **b.** doesn't live   **c.** is no live

5. Mary _____ with her husband, Bill.

   a. live   **b.** is live   **c.** lives

6. Steve _____ at a university.

   a. work   **b.** works   **c.** working

7. Jessica and Tim _____ at home.

   a. doesn't work   **b.** no work   **c.** don't work

8. Jeremy _____ computer games.

   a. likes   **b.** like   **c.** is like

EXERCISE 4: Simple Present Statements: Affirmative

Complete the sentences. Use the correct form of the verbs from the box.

| drive | like | play | report | sing | teach | ~~write~~ |

1. Mark is a writer. He ___*writes*___ novels.

2. Jessica is a news reporter. She _____ the news.

3. Steve is a teacher. He _____ journalism.

4. Nick surfs the Internet a lot. He _____ computers.

5. Kelly is a bus driver. She _____ a bus.

6. Shakira is a singer. She _____ in Spanish and English.

7. Ronaldo and Mario are soccer players. They _____ soccer.

EXERCISE 5: Simple Present Statements: Negative

Complete the sentences. Use negative verbs.

1. We want pizza, but we ___*don't want*___ dessert.

2. The restaurant has spaghetti, but it _____ fish.

3. I speak Spanish, but I _____ Portuguese.

4. Kelly and Ken need a computer, but they _____ a TV.

5. We like coffee, but we _____ tea.

6. My sister wants a dog, but she _____ a cat.

7. You have mistakes in Exercise 1, but you _____ mistakes in Exercise 2.

8. Jack teaches on Mondays, but he _____ on Tuesdays.

9. It rains a lot in Seattle, but it _____ a lot in Los Angeles.

EXERCISE 6: Simple Present Statements: Affirmative and Negative

Look at the pictures. Write true statements about yourself.

1.

eat breakfast

I eat breakfast. OR *I don't eat breakfast.*

2.

drink coffee

_____

3.

read newspapers

_____

4.

surf the Internet

_____

5.

watch TV

_____

6.

study a lot

_____

EXERCISE 7: Simple Present Statements: Affirmative and Negative

Write the correct verb forms. Use the verbs in parentheses.

I _____have_____ a brother and a sister. My sister _____ like me, but my
1. (have)   2. (look)

brother _____ like me or my sister. She and I _____ brown hair
3. (not look)   4. (have)

and brown eyes. My brother _____ black hair and blue eyes. My sister and
5. (have)

I both _____. My sister _____ in an office. I _____ in a
6. (work)   7. (work)   8. (work)

library. My brother _____. He _____ to school, and on weekends he
9. (not work)   10. (go)

_____ cars. He _____ cars, but he _____ school. At work
11. (fix)   12. (love)   13. (not love)

and at school, we _____ English, but we _____ English at home. At
14. (speak)   15. (not speak)

home we _____ Spanish. That's because my parents _____ from the
16. (speak)   17. (not come)

United States. My father _____ from Peru and my mother _____ from
18. (come)   19. (come)

Mexico. My mother _____ English and Spanish, but my father _____
20. (speak)   21. (not speak)

English.

EXERCISE 8: Editing

*Correct the description of Judy's family. There are ten mistakes. The first mistake is
already corrected. Find and correct nine more.*

                    lives

My brother, Ken, ~~live~~ with my parents. They lives in a big house. My father have

a new car. He cleans his car every day. Ken not have a new car. His car is old. It don't

run, but he love it. My mother no love cars. She love her garden. She work in it every

Saturday and Sunday. I doesn't see my family often, but we talk on the weekends.

EXERCISE 9: Personal Writing

*Write about a friend or family member. Use the verbs **like**, **live**, **speak**, and **work**.*

EXAMPLE: *My sister lives in Santa Cruz. She works in a supermarket. She speaks Spanish, but
she doesn't speak English. She likes ice cream, but she doesn't like pizza.*

1. _____

2. _____

3. _____

4. _____

UNIT **11** Simple Present: *Yes / No* Questions

EXERCISE 1: Text Completion

Complete the conversation. Use the words from the box. Don't look at your Student Book.

Do	doesn't	flat screen	~~need~~	sale	want
Does	fix	Josh and I	off	they do	you

AMANDA: Uh . . . Steve, that TV is pretty old. Do you

_____*need*_____ a new one? Do you want a
   1.

_____ TV?
   2.

STEVE: No, I don't think so. This old TV works very well.

AMANDA: How about a smart phone? Do you

_____ a smart phone? _____
   3.   4.

use our smart phones all the time.

STEVE: Not really. Why?

AMANDA: There's a huge _____ at Goodbuys. It
   5.

starts today.

STEVE: Goodbuys? _____ you mean the store on
   6.

Main Street?

AMANDA: Uh-huh. Everything is 30 percent _____.
   7.

They have some great deals.

STEVE: I don't need anything. People have too many things.

AMANDA: Well, what about Jessica? _____ she
   8.

need anything? Does she have a GPS? They're really

helpful. Do Tim, Jeremy, or Ben want anything?

SHOP AT
GOODBUYS!
SALE Starts today
ALL TVs, DVDs,
phones, stereos
30% OFF
HURRY WHILE THINGS LAST!

(continued on next page)

STEVE: I don't know. Amanda, why are you telling me about Goodbuys? Do

_____ work there?
9.

AMANDA: Actually, I do. I'm a new manager.

STEVE: Really? That's great. Wait a second. Do they _____ things?
10.

AMANDA: Yes, _____. The service department is great.
11.

STEVE: Well, that sounds good. My radio _____ work.
12.

AMANDA: Uh . . . Steve. Is that the radio?

STEVE: Yes.

AMANDA: Steve! That radio is older than all of our technicians. I'm not sure they can

fix it.

EXERCISE 2: Vocabulary

Answer the questions. Put a check (✓) below the answer that is true for you.

Do you have . . .	Yes, I do.	No, I don't.
1. . . . a computer?		
2. . . . a flat screen TV?		
3. . . . a smart phone?		
4. . . . a cell phone?		
5. . . . a case for your phone?		
6. . . . a GPS?		
7. . . . a radio?		
8. . . . a lot of computer games?		

EXERCISE 3: Simple Present: *Yes / No* Questions and Short Answers

Match the questions for Jessica with the answers.

Jessica   Ben

_c_ **1.** Do your children clean their rooms?		**a.** No, he doesn't.
_____ **2.** Do you help your children with their homework?		**b.** Yes, she does.
_____ **3.** Does your family eat dinner together?		~~c.~~ No, they don't.
_____ **4.** Does your husband drive to work?		**d.** Yes, we do.
_____ **5.** Does your sister teach at a university?		**e.** Yes, I do.

EXERCISE 4: Simple Present: *Yes / No* Questions

Complete the questions for Ben. Use **do** *or* **does**.

1. _____Does_____ your father play basketball with you?

2. _____ your brother and sister have homework?

3. _____ your parents help you with your homework?

4. _____ your mother drive you to school?

5. _____ you visit your grandparents on the weekend?

6. _____ your grandparents enjoy your visits?

EXERCISE 5: Simple Present: *Yes / No* Questions and Short Answers

Match the questions and answers.

_d_ **1.** Do you sleep every day?		**a.** No, it doesn't.
_____ **2.** Do people in Japan speak Japanese?		**b.** Yes, it does.
_____ **3.** Does it snow in Canada?		**c.** No, I don't.
_____ **4.** Do you read novels in English?		~~d.~~ Yes, I do.
_____ **5.** Does the sun shine at night?		**e.** No, they don't.
_____ **6.** Do teachers do homework?		**f.** Yes, they do.

EXERCISE 6: Simple Present: Short Answers

Look at the chart. Answer the questions. Use short answers.

With their smart phones do they . . . ?	Ken	Judy	Nick	Amy
check email	yes	yes	no	yes
play computer games	yes	no	yes	yes
listen to music	no	no	yes	no
take photos	no	yes	yes	yes
send text messages	yes	no	no	yes

1. Does Ken check email? _Yes, he does._

2. Does Ken listen to music? _No, he doesn't._

3. Does Amy listen to music? _____

4. Do Nick and Judy send text messages? _____

5. Does Judy play computer games? _____

6. Do Nick and Amy play computer games? _____

7. Does Judy check email? _____

Now complete the sentences about yourself.

8. Do you listen to music on your smart phone? _____

9. Do you play computer games on your smart phone? _____

EXERCISE 7: Simple Present: *Yes / No* Questions

Read the statements. Write **yes** / **no** *questions in the simple present. Use the words in parentheses.*

1. Jeremy doesn't play baseball.

   (basketball?) _Does he play basketball?_

2. Jessica doesn't work on Saturday.

   (on Sunday?) _____

3. Mark doesn't speak Spanish.

   (Japanese?) _____

4. Tim and Jessica don't have a flat screen TV.

(computer?) _____

5. Judy doesn't know Amanda.

(Kathy?) _____

6. Mary and Bill don't need a new GPS.

(a new TV?) _____

7. The store doesn't fix flat screen TVs.

(cameras?) _____

8. I don't speak English at home.

(Portuguese?) _____

EXERCISE 8: Simple Present: *Yes / No* Questions and Short Answers

Write questions. Then write short answers. Use the information in parentheses and the simple present.

1. A: _Does Kathy like electronics?_____

   B: _Yes, she does._____ (Kathy likes electronics.)

2. A: _____

   B: _____ (The store doesn't have a service department.)

3. A: _____

   B: _____ (Steve knows a good electronics store.)

4. A: _____

   B: _____ (You don't like computer games.)

5. A: _____

   B: _____ (Bob's Electronics has great deals.)

6. A: _____

   B: _____ (Nick spends lot of time on the computer.)

7. A: _____

   B: _____ (It doesn't cost a lot to send text messages.)

(continued on next page)

8. **A:** _____

   B: _____ (Judy doesn't want a gift.)

9. **A:** _____

   B: _____ (Steve uses his smart phone for a lot of

   things.)

EXERCISE 9: Simple Present: Statements and *Yes / No* Questions

Complete the statements and **yes** / **no** *questions in the simple present. Use the words in parentheses. Use* **do** *or* **does** *where needed.*

ANNIE: _____*We want*_____ a gift for our brother.
         1. (we / want)

SALESPERSON: _____ computer games?
         2. (he / play)

BEN: No, he doesn't.

SALESPERSON: _____ to CDs?
         3. (your brother / listen)

ANNIE: Yeah. _____ a good idea.
         4. (that / be)

SALESPERSON: What kind of music? _____ classical?
         5. (you / like)

ANNIE: Yeah. _____ classical music.
         6. (I / love)

BEN: But _____ classical music. _____ a jazz
         7. (Jeremy / not like)   **8. (you / have)**

CD? _____ jazz.
    9. (Jeremy / love)

EXERCISE 10: Editing

Correct the conversations. There are eight mistakes. The first mistake is already corrected. Find and correct seven more.

      Do you
1. **A:** ~~You~~ know Jeremy?

   B: No. Who is he?

2. **A:** Does your mother has a smart phone?

   B: Yes, she is.

3. **A:** The three stores do have great deals?

   B: One store have great deals. The other two are expensive.

4. A: *Focus on Grammar* have a lot of grammar practice?

   B: Yes, it has.

5. A: Do you and the other students like this book?

   B: No, we don't like.

EXERCISE 11: Personal Writing

Write **yes** / **no** *questions to ask at an electronics store in your town. Try to use* **do** *and* **does** *in your questions.*

   EXAMPLE: *Do you sell smart phones?*

   1. _____

   2. _____

   3. _____

   4. _____

EXERCISE 1: Text Completion

Complete the conversation. Use the words from the box. Don't look at your Student Book.

do	go	is	off	stay up	what
does	have	~~like~~	start	time	Why

JEREMY: So how do you _____ like _____ the
1.

United States?

YOSHIO: I like it a lot. But it's really different from

Japan.

JEREMY: What _____ you mean?
2.

YOSHIO: I think in Japan we stay up later.

JEREMY: What time do Japanese people _____ to bed?
3.

YOSHIO: Students _____ till midnight or later. And my father stays
4.

up till 1:00 or 2:00 A.M.

JEREMY: Really? _____ does he stay up so late? What
5.

_____ he do?
6.

YOSHIO: He's a businessman. He meets clients in the evening.

JEREMY: What _____ do people get up in Japan?
7.

YOSHIO: Oh, maybe 7:00 or 7:30.

JEREMY: That's pretty much like here. . . . What else _____ different?
8.

YOSHIO: Well, in the United States, most people wear their shoes in the house. In Japan

we take our shoes _____.
9.

JEREMY: Wow! That's different. . . . So _____ do you like best about
10.

the United States?

YOSHIO: People here are open and friendly. I have a lot of friends here.

Jeremy: That's good. Hey, we _____ calculus!
11.

Yoshio: Uh-oh! What time does it _____?
12.

Jeremy: Two o'clock. It's almost 2:00 now.

Yoshio: OK, let's go.

EXERCISE 2: Vocabulary

Match the questions and answers.

_d_ **1.** What time do you get up?

_____ **2.** Where do you have breakfast?

_____ **3.** When do you start work?

_____ **4.** What do you have for lunch?

_____ **5.** Why does your mother go to bed early?

_____ **6.** Who do you have dinner with?

_____ **7.** How late do you stay up?

_____ **8.** What do you take off?

a. After my morning English class.

b. A sandwich.

c. Till midnight or later.

d. At about 7:00 A.M.

e. My parents and my brother.

f. My shoes.

g. At home.

h. Because she gets up early.

EXERCISE 3: Simple Present: *Wh-* Questions

Put the words in the correct order. Write questions.

1. you / to school / do / Where / go / ? _Where do you go to school?_

2. goes / with you / Who / to school / ? _____

3. you / do / to school / How / get ? _____

4. What / study / you / in school / do / ? _____

5. your brother / to school / Why / early / does / go / ? _____

6. home / get / your brother / What time / does / ? _____

7. play / you / do / tennis / When / ? _____

Look at the examples. Write the times.

It's seven o'clock.
It's seven.

It's five after seven.
It's seven-oh-five.

It's a quarter after seven.
It's seven fifteen.

It's half past seven.
It's seven thirty.

It's seven thirty-five.
It's twenty-five to eight.

It's a quarter to eight.
It's seven forty-five.

1. 7:40   *It's seven forty,* OR *It's twenty to eight.* _____

2. 7:10 _____

3. 3:02 _____

4. 4:40 _____

5. 8:50 _____

6. 7:55 _____

7. 11:00 _____

8. 1:30 _____

9. 2:15 _____

10. 6:45 _____

11. 10:25 _____

12. 3:35 _____

EXERCISE 5: Simple Present: *Wh-* Questions

Write questions about the underlined expressions. Use **what, what time, where, who,** *or* **why.**

1. **A:** _What time do you wake up?_

   B: I wake up <u>at 7:30</u>.

2. **A:** _____

   B: My mother? <u>She's a nurse</u>.

3. **A:** _____

   B: <u>Because</u> I like jazz. It's my favorite music.

4. **A:** _____

   B: Dinner? Usually <u>at 6:00</u>.

5. **A:** _____

   B: <u>Because</u> he starts work at 5:00 A.M.

6. **A:** _____

   B: Two of my cousins live <u>in New York</u>. My other cousins live <u>in different cities</u>.

7. **A:** _____

   B: <u>My uncle</u> owns the restaurant.

EXERCISE 6: Editing

Correct the conversation. There are eight mistakes. The first two mistakes are already corrected. Find and correct six more.

              does   start

YUKO: What time English class <s>starts</s>?

OMAR: At 1:00.

YUKO: What time class finish?

OMAR: At 2:30.

YUKO: What means *dislike*?

OMAR: It means "not like."

YUKO: How you say this word?

OMAR: I don't know.

(continued on next page)

Yuko: Do the teacher teach every day?

Omar: No. She doesn't teach on Friday.

Yuko: What have we for homework?

Omar: Page 97.

Yuko: Why does Elena know all the answers?

Omar: She study a lot.

EXERCISE 7: Personal Writing

*Write four questions to ask a classmate. Use **Wh-** words to find out about his or her everyday life.*

Example: *Where do you have breakfast?*

1. _____

2. _____

3. _____

4. _____

13 Simple Present: *Be* and *Have*

EXERCISE 1: Text Completion

Complete the conversation. Use the words from the box. Don't look at your Student Book.

are	don't	have	look like	She's	thin
dark hair	has	is	pregnant	tall	~~You're~~

RICK: _____You're_____ in Music Appreciation 101, aren't
　　　　　　　1.
　　　you?

JUDY: Uh-huh . . .

RICK: Could you please give these tickets to Sonia Jones?

　　　　　_____ in your music class.
　　　　　　　　2.

JUDY: Sure. But I _____ know her. What does
　　　　　　　　　　　3.
　　　she _____?
　　　　　　4.

RICK: Well, she has _____ and dark eyes.
　　　　　　　　　　5.

JUDY: Half the women _____ dark hair and dark
　　　　　　　　　　　6.
　　　eyes. And there _____ 100 students in my
　　　　　　　　　　7.
　　　class.

RICK: She's _____ and thin.
　　　　　　　8.

JUDY: OK, but a lot of women are tall and _____.
　　　　　　　　　　　　　　　9.

RICK: She's in her early twenties.

JUDY: Rick! Almost everyone at school _____
　　　　　　　　　　　　　　10.
　　　20-something. Is there something unusual about her?

RICK: She _____ two heads.
　　　　　　　11.

JUDY: Rick!

RICK: Sonia's eight months _____.
　　　　　　　　　　　　12.

JUDY: Why didn't you say so?

EXERCISE 2: Vocabulary

Look at the pictures. Complete the sentences. Use **is, isn't, are, aren't, has, doesn't have, have,** *or* **don't have.**

Mike   Ben   Susan   Liam   Peter   Jen   Cheryl   Holly

1. Cheryl _____is_____ heavy. She _doesn't have_ dark hair.

2. Liam _____ short. He _____ curly hair.

3. Susan and Cheryl _____ tall. They _____ curly blonde hair.

4. Mike _____ tall. He _____ straight blond hair.

5. Ben and Holly _____ thin. They _____ blond hair.

6. Susan _____ pregnant. She _____ straight blond hair.

7. Peter _____ average weight. He _____ curly dark hair.

8. Jen _____ pregnant. She _____ black hair.

EXERCISE 3: *Be* and *Have*: Statements

Complete the sentences about yourself. Use **'m, 'm not, have,** *or* **don't have.**

1. I _'m OR 'm not_ divorced.

2. I _____ one brother and one sister.

3. I _____ 19 years old.

4. I _____ hazel eyes.

5. I _____ curly hair.

6. I _____ a university student.

7. I _____ a job.

8. I _____ tall.

9. I _____ from Mexico.

10. I _____ light brown hair.

Complete the description. Use the correct forms of **be** or **have**.

These ___are___ pictures of Bono and his band. The name of the band
                1.

_____ U2. Bono _____ the singer in the band.
     2.   3.

Bono _____ the singer's real name. His real name _____ Paul
            4.   5.

Hewson. He _____ from Dublin, Ireland. He _____ one brother, but he
                  6.   7.

_____ any sisters.
     8.

Bono _____ married to Alison Stewart. They _____ four children—
            9.   10.

two daughters and two sons. They _____ a home in Dublin. Their children's names
                                       11.

_____ Jordan, Memphis Eve, Elijah, and John Abraham.
     12.

Write questions about Bono. Use the words in parentheses and the correct forms of **be**
or **have**. Use **do** or **does** where needed.

1. (Who / the man in the pictures / ?) _Who's the man in the pictures?_____

2. (Bono / in a band / ?) _Is Bono in a band?_____

3. (What / the name of Bono's band / ?) _____

4. (Bono / a violinist / ?) _____

5. (What / Bono's real name / ?) _____

6. (Where / he from / ?) _____

7. (he / any brothers or sisters / ?) _____

(continued on next page)

8. (he / married / ?) _____

9. (they / children / ?) _____

10. (Where / they / a home / ?) _____

Correct the conversation. There are eight mistakes. The first mistake is already corrected. Find and correct seven more.

     What's

A: ~~What~~ your name?

B: Alice.

A: How old have you?

B: I have twenty-four.

A: You have a big family?

B: Yes, I do. I have three sisters and four brothers.

A: Where do you live?

B: My home near here. It's on Center Street.

A: Is big?

B: No. It small. I live alone. My family lives in another city.

A: Have you a job?

B: No. I study at a university.

Write a description of yourself.

    EXAMPLE: *I'm in my twenties. I have straight black hair and brown eyes. I'm not short, but I'm not tall. I'm average weight.*

1. _____

2. _____

3. _____

4. _____

EXERCISE 1: Text Completion

Complete the conversation. Use the words from the box. Don't look at your Student Book.

always	ever	I'm	often	Sometimes	~~usually~~
always have	have	I sometimes	Rarely	times	usually go

JOSH: How's it going, Steve? You look kind of tired.

STEVE: Well, things are OK, but I *am* a little tired.

JOSH: Any idea why?

STEVE: Maybe I'm not getting enough sleep.

JOSH: How much do you get?

STEVE: Oh, about six hours a night.

JOSH: What time do you go to bed?

STEVE: I ____*usually*____ stay up till 12:30 or 1:00. And
      1.
I get up at 6:30 or 7:00.

JOSH: Do you _____ sleep late?
            2.

STEVE: _____—on the weekend.
  3.

JOSH: And I hear you _____ fast food for lunch.
          4.

STEVE: And _____ skip breakfast.
     5.

JOSH: So you don't eat three meals a day?

STEVE: _____. I'm usually in a hurry in the morning. So I skip breakfast.
     6.

JOSH: Not good, my friend. What about lunch and dinner?

STEVE: I always _____ a good dinner. But lunch . . . well, _____ always in
          7.   **8.**
a hurry then. So I _____ to a fast-food place near the university. I know
              9.
fast food isn't _____ healthy.
        10.

JOSH: Hmm. Not enough sleep. No breakfast. Fast food for lunch. You're living

dangerously.

(continued on next page)

STEVE: Maybe. But I have one good habit. I exercise.

JOSH: Great. How _____?
                          11.

STEVE: Two or three _____ a year.
                          12.

EXERCISE 2: Vocabulary

Complete the crossword puzzle.

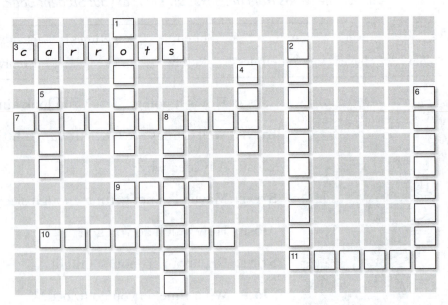

ACROSS

3.

7.

9.

10.

11.

DOWN

1.

2.

4.

5.

6.

8.

EXERCISE 3: Adverbs of Frequency: *Be* and Other Verbs

Complete the sentences so they are true for you. Use **always, usually, often, sometimes, rarely,** *or* **never.**

1. I _____ wake up on time.

2. I _____ get up early.

3. I _____ go to bed very late.

4. I'm _____ tired in the afternoon.

5. I _____ have vegetables for dinner.

6. I'm _____ hungry in the morning.

7. I _____ exercise in the morning.

8. I _____ eat dinner alone.

EXERCISE 4: Adverbs of Frequency: Word Order

Put the words in the correct order. Write sentences. Don't change any capitalization.

1. late / sleep / never / I / . _I never sleep late._ _____

2. does / Steve / exercise / often / not / . _____

3. rarely / donuts / Bill / eats / . _____

4. here / It / snows / sometimes / . _____

5. Mary / not / usually / busy / is / . _____

6. Cairo / often / is / It / hot / in / . _____

EXERCISE 5: Adverbs of Frequency

Rewrite the sentences. Replace the underlined words. Use **always, often, sometimes, rarely,** *or* **never.**

1. I drink coffee <u>every day</u>. _I always drink coffee._ _____

2. I play soccer <u>one or two times a month</u>. _____

3. I am late for class <u>one or two times a year</u>. _____

4. The food at that restaurant is <u>not</u> good. _____

5. Jennifer sees a play <u>one time a year</u>. _____

6. Robert goes to the movies <u>two times a week</u>. _____

EXERCISE 6: Adverbs of Frequency

Look at the pictures. Write a sentence about each person. Use **always, usually, sometimes,** *or* **never** *and the words in parentheses.*

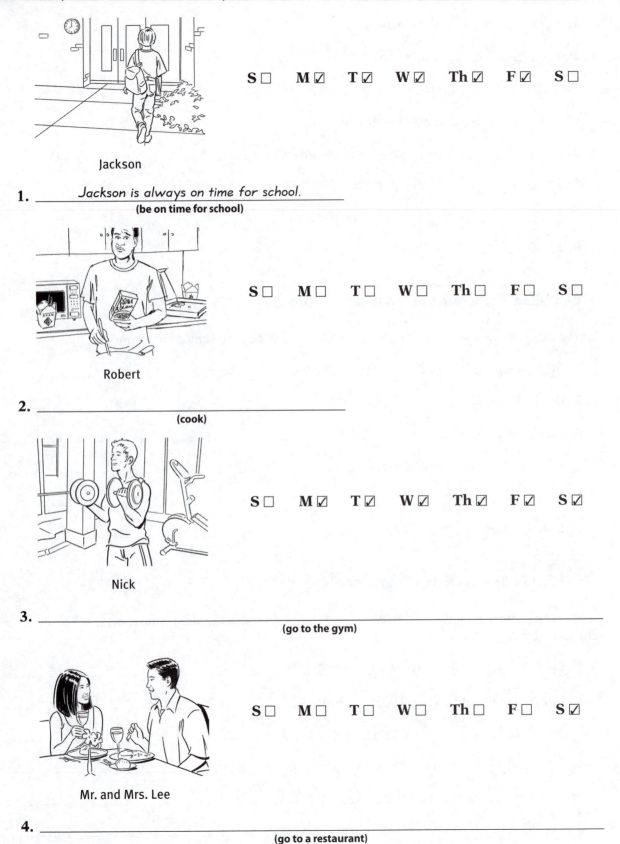

S ☐   M ☑   T ☑   W ☑   Th ☑   F ☑   S ☐

Jackson

1. _____ Jackson is always on time for school. _____
   (be on time for school)

S ☐   M ☐   T ☐   W ☐   Th ☐   F ☐   S ☐

Robert

2. _____
   (cook)

S ☐   M ☑   T ☑   W ☑   Th ☑   F ☑   S ☑

Nick

3. _____
   (go to the gym)

S ☐   M ☐   T ☐   W ☐   Th ☐   F ☐   S ☑

Mr. and Mrs. Lee

4. _____
   (go to a restaurant)

S ☑ M ☑ T ☑ W ☑ Th ☑ F ☑ S ☑

Ruth

5. _____

(eat lunch)

EXERCISE 7: Questions with *Ever* and *How often*

*Write a question for each answer. Use **ever** or **how often**.*

1. A: _How often do you go dancing?_____

   B: Go dancing? I never go dancing.

2. A: _____

   B: Yes, I do. I go to the theater two or three times a year.

3. A: _____

   B: No, they don't. My children never eat sweets.

4. A: _____

   B: The radio? I listen to the radio every day.

5. A: _____

   B: No, never. I never eat fast food.

6. A: _____

   B: Tim? He cooks fish one or two times a week.

7. A: _____

   B: Yes. I'm usually home on the weekend.

EXERCISE 8: Editing

Correct the email. There are six mistakes. The first mistake is already corrected. Find and correct five more.

Subj: My schedule
Date: Friday, September 15
From: BJones@AU.edu
To: SamD92@AU.edu

Hi, Sam,

    Here is my schedule. I ~~usually am~~ *am usually* busy on Monday evenings. I go often to the gym,

or I play basketball. (Do ever you play basketball?) On Fridays always I exercise too.

I go dancing at the club! On Wednesdays and Thursdays I sometimes work late, but

I'm often free on Tuesdays. I finish work usually at 5:30. Do you want to meet at

Vincenzo's Italian Restaurant at 6:30 on Tuesday? The food there is good always.

Bob

EXERCISE 9: Personal Writing

Write four sentences about what you **always, usually, often, sometimes, rarely,** *or* **never** *do.*

EXAMPLE: *I always wake up at 6:00 A.M.*

1. _____

2. _____

3. _____

4. _____

UNIT 15 Present Progressive: Statements

EXERCISE 1: Text Completion

Complete the email. Use the words from the box. Don't look at your Student Book.

are	not
~~happy~~	not working
He's	sitting
I'm	texting
is	They're
living	were

Dear Lauren,

I was so surprised and _____*happy*_____ to get your email. Yes, I'm the Jessica Beck
                                    1.

from Seattle High School. And of course I remember you. We _____
                                                              2.

together in math for four years.

   I'm _____ in Redmond with my husband and children. Here are some
        3.

photos of us.

   Tim is my husband. _____ wearing the gray sweatshirt. He's
                         4.

_____ next to my brother, Steve. _____ watching a ball
      5.   6.

game. They're _____ smiling because their team _____
                  7.   8.

losing. I'm sure you remember Steve. Believe it or not, he's a professor now.

(continued on next page)

My son Jeremy is in the chair. He's fifteen. He's _____ friends. He's a
9.

great kid. Annie and Ben _____ playing cards. Annie is ten, and Ben is
10.

seven. They keep us busy.

In this photo _____ standing between my parents. They're
11.

_____ now. Mom is happy, but Dad misses work.
12.

Please call as soon as you get to Washington. My cell phone number is

555–460–9878. I'll meet you at the airport.

Love from your long-lost friend,

Jessica

EXERCISE 2: Vocabulary

Match the parts of sentences on the left and right.

__e__ **1.** She's wearing boots because

____ **2.** She's sitting on the bus because

____ **3.** They're watching TV because

____ **4.** They're losing because

____ **5.** They're standing in line at a restaurant because

____ **6.** She's smiling because

a. the best player isn't playing.

b. they're waiting for a table.

c. she's texting her friend something funny.

d. she's going to school.

e. it's snowing.

f. their team is playing.

EXERCISE 3: Base Form and Verb + *-ing*

Write the **-ing** *form of the verbs.*

Base Form	Base Form + *-ing*	Base Form	Base Form + *-ing*
1. ask	*asking*	**7.** look	_____
2. close	_____	**8.** listen	_____
3. do	_____	**9.** move	_____
4. stop	_____	**10.** open	_____
5. enjoy	_____	**11.** run	_____
6. fix	_____	**12.** try	_____

EXERCISE 4: Present Progressive: Affirmative Statements

Look at the picture. Complete the paragraph. Use the verbs from the box and the present progressive.

| cook | help | listen | ~~play~~ | read | wash | work | write |

Things are happening at the Olson house today. Annie and Ben _____*are playing*_____

1.

video games. Jeremy and his friend _____ to music and

2.

_____ magazines. Grandma _____ dinner. Grandpa

3.   **4.**

_____ the dishes and Tim _____ Grandpa. Jessica

5.   **6.**

_____ at the computer. She _____ an email to her

7.   **8.**

friend.

EXERCISE 5: Present Progressive: Affirmative and Negative Statements

Write true sentences about yourself. Use the words in parentheses and the present progressive.

1. (I / wear / a jacket / right now)

   I'm wearing a jacket right now. OR *I'm not wearing a jacket right now.*

2. (I / wear / glasses / right now)

_____

3. (I / text / right now)

_____

4. (I / sit / in my bedroom / right now)

_____

5. (I / eat / right now)

_____

6. (I / sit / with my friend / right now)

_____

7. (I / drink / water / right now)

_____

8. (I / look / at a computer / right now)

_____

EXERCISE 6: Editing

Correct the postcard. There are eight mistakes. The first mistake is already corrected. Find and correct seven more.

> It's
> Hello from Seattle. ~~It~~ raining right now, but we have fun. Jenny and I are sit in a restaurant. I eating lunch. The food here in Seattle is good. Jenny no is eating. She drink coffee. We aren't talk. Jenny's read the newspaper. I hope you're fine.
>
> Love,
> Amy
>
> Mom and Dad
> 40 McPherson St.
> Allawah NSW 2218
> Australia

EXERCISE 7: Personal Writing

Write sentences about what is happening around you right now.

EXAMPLE: My roommate is listening to music.

1. _____

2. _____

3. _____

4. _____

EXERCISE 1: Text Completion

Complete the conversations. Use the words from the box. Don't look at your Student Book.

are	babysitting	How's	Is he	studying	watching
around	baking	~~Is~~	listening	They're	with

TIM: Hi, hon. Happy anniversary!

JESSICA: Thanks. You too.

TIM: Everyone OK? _____*Is*_____ Jeremy
                1.
_____ Ben and Annie?
       2.

JESSICA: No. Jeremy's at a basketball game with Steve.

TIM: Oh. Is Mrs. Brown _____?
                 3.

JESSICA: No. Her granddaughter Kelly Brown is.

[Later—Jessica calls Kelly.]

KELLY: Hello?

JESSICA: Hi, Kelly. This is Mrs. Olson. _____
                            4.
everything? Are the children _____
                            5.
to you?

KELLY: Sure. Everything's great.

JESSICA: So _____ you helping Ben
           6.
_____ his math? _____
    7.   8.
doing his homework?

KELLY: No, not now. He's _____ cookies. He
                      9.
says he's the family baker.

JESSICA: He is? Well, is Annie _____ for her
                          10.
science test?

KELLY: I think so. Her friend Gail is here. They're in Annie's room. It's quiet.

_____ probably studying.
     11.

JESSICA: Hmm. Well, I'm sure they are, but can you check?

KELLY: OK, Mrs. Olson. Look. Don't worry. Everything's cool. Enjoy your anniversary.

JESSICA: Thanks, Kelly. We'll be back _____ 10:00.
                                           12.

KELLY: See you then. Bye.

EXERCISE 2: Vocabulary

Match the questions and answers.

___f___ **1.** Is Tom worrying about the children?

_____ **2.** Is Ben getting a haircut?

_____ **3.** Are the kids making a mess in the house?

_____ **4.** Are they celebrating their anniversary?

_____ **5.** Are you babysitting?

_____ **6.** Is Kelly Brown cutting Annie's hair?

_____ **7.** Is Jeremy helping Ben with his homework?

a. No, they aren't. They're playing outside.

b. Yes, I am. I'm playing with the kids right now.

c. No, she's not. She's babysitting.

d. No, he isn't. He's at a basketball game with Steve.

e. Yes, they are. They're eating at a restaurant right now.

f. No, he isn't. They're with his mother.

g. Yes, he is. He's at the barber shop.

EXERCISE 3: Present Progressive: Short Answers

Answer the questions. Write true short answers.

1. Are you listening to music? _Yes, I am._ OR _No, I'm not._ _____

2. Is it raining? _____

3. Is the sun shining? _____

4. Are you doing your homework? _____

5. Are your friends helping you with your homework? _____

6. Are you having fun? _____

7. Are you working hard? _____

8. Are you eating a snack? _____

EXERCISE 4: Present Progressive: *Yes / No* Questions and Short Answers

Write questions. Then complete the short answers. Use the information in parentheses and the present progressive.

1. A: <u>Is Susan writing a letter?</u>

    B: Yes, <u>she is.</u>   (Susan's writing a letter.)

2. A: _____

    B: No, _____ (He's not sleeping in his bedroom.)

3. A: _____

    B: Yes, _____ (The Smiths are celebrating.)

4. A: _____

    B: No, _____ (Ben isn't getting a haircut.)

5. A: _____

    B: No, _____ (The children aren't cleaning the kitchen.)

6. A: _____

    B: Yes, _____ (Paula's drinking coffee with milk.)

EXERCISE 5: Present Progressive: *Yes / No* Questions and Short Answers

Look at the picture. Write questions. Use the words in parentheses and the present progressive. Then write short answers.

1. (Jessica and Tim / eat at a restaurant)

   Are Jessica and Tim eating at a restaurant?   No, they aren't.

2. (Jessica / wear a hat)

   Is Jessica wearing a hat?   No, she isn't. OR No, she's not.

3. (Jessica / cook dinner)

_____   _____

4. (the cat / wear a hat)

_____   _____

5. (Ben and Annie / play cards)

_____   _____

6. (Jeremy / listen to music)

_____   _____

7. (Tim / write a letter)

_____   _____

(continued on next page)

8. (the cat / sit on the floor)

_____   _____

9. (the cat / read)

_____   _____

Complete the conversation. Write statements and **yes** / **no** questions. Use the words in parentheses and the present progressive.

GAIL: _____ Is your mother baking _____?
            1. (your mother / bake)

ANNIE: No, that's my brother. _____ cookies.
                   2. (he / make)

GAIL: _____ in the dining room?
     3. (your parents / eat)

ANNIE: No, that's Kelly, the babysitter. _____ dinner at a
                          4. (my parents / have)

restaurant. It's their anniversary.

GAIL: What about Jeremy? _____?
                  5. (he / sleep)

ANNIE: No, he isn't. _____ a basketball game with our uncle.
           6. (he / watch)

Correct the conversations. There are ten mistakes. The first mistake is already corrected. Find and correct nine more.

         making

1. A: Are you ~~make~~ a mess?

   B: No, I not.

2. A: Your sister helping you with your homework?

   B: Yes, she's.

3. A: Is Mr. Olson work?

   B: No, he isn't. He's eat lunch.

4. A: Is sleeping Kelly?

   B: No, she's not. She watching a DVD with her friend.

5. A: Is Chris and Lee babysitting?

   B: Yes, they're.

EXERCISE 8: Personal Writing

Write four **yes** / **no** *questions to ask classmates. Find out what they are doing now. Then send them an email with your questions.*

EXAMPLE: *Ana, are you surfing the Internet right now?*

1. _____

2. _____

3. _____

4. _____

Present Progressive: *Wh-* Questions

EXERCISE 1: Text Completion

Complete the conversation. Use the words from the box. Don't look at your Student Book.

are	By	driving	planning	traveling	~~What's~~
are you	doing	He's	This	What	Who

MARK: Hello?

NICK: Hey, little brother . . . _____*what's*_____

       _{1.}

       happening?

MARK: Nick? Is it really you?

NICK: Yep. _____ is your big brother.

       _{2.}

MARK: I can't believe it. Why _____

       _{3.}

       you calling me? You hate phones.

NICK: I know . . . I emailed you, but you didn't answer.

MARK: _____ are you doing? Are you still

       _{4.}

       in Kenya?

NICK: Nope. I'm back in the United States. I'm on my

       way to a job interview in Denver.

MARK: In Colorado? Wow! Are you

       _____ to leave Kenya?

       _{5.}

NICK: I don't know. It's possible.

MARK: How are you _____? I think I

       _{6.}

       hear a car engine.

NICK: _____ car. You still have good ears.

       _{7.}

       Do you remember my old friend Jerry Gomez?

       He's _____ me to Denver.

       _{8.}

MARK: Sure I remember him. What's Jerry

_____ these days?

　　　　　　　　　9.

NICK: _____ teaching at a college in

　　　　10.

Colorado.

MARK: Can you come to Seattle?

NICK: That's my plan. I'll be there next week.

* * * * *

JUDY: Why _____ smiling?

　　　　　　　11.

_____ was on the phone?

　12.

MARK: My brother Nick—the interesting one.

EXERCISE 2: Vocabulary

Complete the sentences with **by bicycle, by bus, by boat, by car, by plane, by subway,**
or **by train.**

1. We're traveling ___by plane___ from Miami to Lima. It's a long trip—about eight

   hours. Right now we're all wearing our seat belts.

2. We're traveling around France _____. We're traveling about 70 kilometers a

   day, but we're stopping in a lot of small villages, and we're getting lots of exercise.

3. We're traveling _____ around the islands. Sometimes it's cool outside, but I

   love to be on the water.

4. I'm traveling to Washington _____ with my 20 classmates. There are lots of

   cars on the road.

5. We're traveling _____ from Tokyo to Kyoto. It's fast, clean, and easy. Some

   people are selling food and drinks.

6. I'm traveling _____ with my girlfriend from Toronto to Vancouver. It's

   beautiful. We're stopping and taking lots of pictures.

7. I'm traveling around New York City _____. It's fast because there are no

   cars, but it's noisy and crowded.

EXERCISE 3: Question Words

Write the correct question words. Use **Who, What, Where, Why,** *or* **How.**

1. ___Where___ ? On the grass by the pond.

2. _____? Jeremy.

3. _____? Listening to music.

4. _____? On a blanket.

5. _____? Because they're hungry.

6. _____? Happy.

7. _____? They're riding bicycles.

8. _____? On a bench.

EXERCISE 4: Present Progressive: *Wh-* Questions and Short Answers

Write questions. Use the words in parentheses and the present progressive. Then find an answer in Exercise 3 for each question. Write short answers.

1. (Where / Mary and Bill / sit / ?)

   ___Where are Mary and Bill sitting?___   ___On a bench.___

2. (Where / the family / have / a picnic / ?)

   _____   _____

3. (What / Jeremy / do / ?)

   _____   _____

4. (Why / Jessica and Tim / eat / ?)

_____   _____

5. (How / everyone / feel / ?)

_____   _____

6. (Where / Jessica and Tim / sit / ?)

_____   _____

7. (Who / listen to / music / ?)

_____   _____

8. (What / Annie and Ben / do ?)

_____   _____

EXERCISE 5: Present Progressive: _Wh-_ Questions

Complete the conversations. Write questions with **where, what, why,** _or_ **who.**

1. A: I'm texting my sister.

   B: _Why are you texting_____ her?

   A: She doesn't like to talk on the phone.

2. A: Shh! I'm talking.

   B: _____ to?

   A: My little brother.

3. A: I'm wearing my nice clothes for the interview.

   B: _____?

   A: A suit and tie.

4. A: Nick isn't traveling alone.

   B: _____ with Nick?

   A: His friend Jerry is.

5. A: Nick's teaching.

   B: _____?

   A: In Kenya.

EXERCISE 6: Editing

Correct the conversations. There are nine mistakes. The first mistake is already corrected. Find and correct eight more.

1. **A:** What ~~you are~~ are you doing?

   B: My homework.

2. **A:** How the people traveling?

   B: With boat.

3. **A:** Why Nick is wearing a suit?

   B: Because he going to a job interview.

4. **A:** What's everything going?

   B: Great. We are have a lot of fun.

5. **A:** Where Nick and Jerry are going?

   B: To Denver.

6. **A:** Who's Jeremy send an email message to?

   B: A friend from school.

EXERCISE 7: Personal Writing

Imagine your friend is at a party. Write questions to text to your friend. Use words such as **who, what, where,** *and* **how** *and the present progressive.*

EXAMPLE: Who are you talking to? What is everyone eating?

1. _____

2. _____

3. _____

4. _____

PART VII

NOUNS; *THIS / THAT / THESE / THOSE; SOME* AND *ANY; ARTICLES; CAN / CAN'T*

UNIT 18 Possessive Nouns; *This / That / These / Those*

EXERCISE 1: Text Completion

Complete the conversation. Use the words from the box. Don't look at your Student Book.

brother's	Kathy's	parents'	that	that's good	This
fit	~~parents~~	roommate's	That's	these	those

MARK: Judy, do I look OK?

JUDY: Yeah. You look really sharp. What's the

occasion?

MARK: I'm having dinner with Kathy and her

_____*parents*_____. It's her _____
      1.   **2.**

anniversary. They're taking us to an expensive

new restaurant, The Water Grill.

JUDY: _____ nice. Is _____
            3.   **4.**

a new sports jacket?

MARK: It's my _____ jacket.
                    5.

JUDY: It's a good _____.
                       6.

MARK: Are _____ suspenders OK?
                 7.

JUDY: Sure. They go well with that tie and _____ shoes.
                                                    8.

MARK: Thanks. Actually they aren't mine. They're my _____. I almost never
                                                            9.

wear a tie or dress shoes.

(continued on next page)

JUDY: Oh yeah? Is *anything* yours?

MARK: Uh-huh. _____ new goatee. It's all
    10.
mine.

JUDY: Oh. I see. You know, that goatee makes you look
like an artist.

MARK: An artist? No kidding. I guess _____.
    11.
Now I need to remember—_____ mom
    12.
is Bea Harlow, and her dad is Lee White.

JUDY: Relax, Mark. Just be yourself. They're going to love you!

EXERCISE 2: Vocabulary

Complete the sentences. Use the words from the box.

belt	dress shoes	~~ring~~	sports jackets	tie
casual shoes	earrings	slacks	~~suspenders~~	

1. Mark likes Jim's __suspenders__.

2. Judy's looking at Kathy's ____ring____.

3. Kathy's _____ are big.

4. Kathy's _____ are white.

5. Mark's _____ is unusual.

6. Mark's _____ are gray.

7. Mark's _____ are black.

8. Mark's _____ isn't a good fit.

9. Jim's _____ is white.

EXERCISE 3: Possessive Nouns

Correct the sentences. Add **'s** or **'** where necessary. The first sentence is already corrected.

1. Jessica's house is big.

2. His parents names are Bill and Mary.

3. Steve apartment is in Seattle.

4. The students tests are on the desk.

5. The teacher book is in her bag.

6. Our daughters husbands are very nice.

7. The children room is on the second floor.

8. My roommate cousins visit her every weekend.

9. Josh tie goes well with his sports jacket.

10. Kathy last name is White.

EXERCISE 4: Possessive 's or Contraction?

Rewrite the sentences where possible. Replace contractions with full forms.

1. Jack's wearing black dress shoes. _Jack is wearing black dress shoes._

2. Who's wearing Mark's sports jacket? _____

3. That's not Sam's shirt. _____

4. The woman's not looking at the slacks. _____

5. Steve's last name is Jones. _____

6. Amanda's wearing new sunglasses. _____

7. It's Ben's tie. _____

8. Mark's nervous about his dinner with Kathy's parents. _____

EXERCISE 5: *This / That / These / Those*

What are the people saying? Complete the conversations. Write questions with **what** *and* **this, that, these,** *or* **those.**

1. A: _What are these?_____

   B: _Those_____ are suspenders.

2. A: _____

   B: _____ are contact lenses.

3. A: _____

   B: I don't know!

4. A: _____

   B: _____ is a blog.

EXERCISE 6: Editing

Correct the conversations. There are six mistakes. The first mistake is already corrected. Find and correct five more.

1. A: Does my ~~brother~~ ^brother's^ jacket look good on me?

   B: Hmm. I'm not sure.

2. A: The women rest room is over there.

   B: Thanks.

3. A: Who's this over there?

   B: That's Ken.

4. A: Look at Mark over there. Does he usually wear ties?

B: No. He's wearing his brother tie. And this isn't Mark's sports jacket either.

5. A: Those earrings look really good on Judy.

B: Yeah. I like that earrings too.

EXERCISE 7: Personal Writing

Write sentences about the clothes of people you know.

EXAMPLE: My father's sports jacket is blue.

1. _____

2. _____

3. _____

4. _____

19 Count and Non-Count Nouns; *Some* and *Any*

EXERCISE 1: Text Completion

Complete the conversations. Use the words from the box. Don't look at your Student Book.

~~a~~	any	breakfast	cup	of	That's
an	banana	coffee	I'm	some	what

JESSICA: Hello, everyone. This morning we're interviewing people about their eating habits . . . Excuse me, sir, do you eat breakfast?

MAN: Yes, more or less.

JESSICA: What do you have?

MAN: I generally have _____*a*_____ bagel and a

          1.

_____ of tea.

    2.

JESSICA: _____ all? Do you have

    3.

_____ juice or anything else to drink?

    4.

MAN: Not usually. Once in a while I have

_____ instead of tea. I'm always in a

    5.

hurry. Bye.

JESSICA: OK. Thanks. Bye.

JESSICA: Now, here's our next person. Ma'am, _____ do you have for breakfast?
                                              6.

WOMAN 1: I never eat _____.
                                7.

JESSICA: Nothing at all?

WOMAN 1: No. _____ on a diet. I'm *always* on a
                     8.
diet.

JESSICA: OK. Thank you . . .

JESSICA: And what about you, ma'am? What do you have for
breakfast?

WOMAN 2: Oh, I usually have a bowl of cereal and

_____ yogurt with fruit—a
         9.

_____, a peach, or _____
         10.   **11.**
orange, or some strawberries. And I have eggs and

toast and a glass _____ juice.
                          12.

JESSICA: Hmm. That sounds healthy.

WOMAN 2: Yes, I always eat a good breakfast.

JESSICA: All right, thanks. Let's see what our next person
says . . .

EXERCISE 2: Vocabulary

Match the words and the pictures. Write the correct letters.

a.

b.

c.

d.

e.

f.

g.

h.

i.

j.

k.

l.

_h_	**1.** salad	___	**5.** eggs	___	**9.** coffee
___	**2.** tuna	___	**6.** bagel	___	**10.** candy
___	**3.** fruit	___	**7.** olives	___	**11.** sandwich
___	**4.** yogurt	___	**8.** toast	___	**12.** cereal

EXERCISE 3: Count and Non-Count Nouns

*Write **a, an,** or **some** before each word.*

_a_	**1.** bagel	___	**9.** fruit	___	**17.** rice
___	**2.** banana	___	**10.** hamburger	___	**18.** sandwich
___	**3.** bread	___	**11.** ice cream	___	**19.** soda
___	**4.** candy	___	**12.** juice	___	**20.** strawberry
___	**5.** cereal	___	**13.** milk	___	**21.** toast
___	**6.** chip	___	**14.** olive	___	**22.** tuna
___	**7.** coffee	___	**15.** orange	___	**23.** water
___	**8.** egg	___	**16.** peach	___	**24.** yogurt

EXERCISE 4: *Some* and *Any*

Complete the sentences. Use **some** or **any**.

1. I don't have _____ any _____ money.

2. I don't want _____ cereal.

3. Do they have _____ tuna?

4. Julie needs _____ coffee.

5. Does he want _____ juice?

6. We want _____ sandwiches.

7. Steve has _____ eggs and a slice of toast.

8. Do you have _____ strawberries?

EXERCISE 5: Quantifiers with Non-Count Nouns

Complete the sentences. Cross out the incorrect word in parentheses.

1. Would you like a (bottle / ~~slice~~ / glass) of water?

2. I have a (bowl / bottle / glass) of iced tea.

3. Here is (some / a bottle of / a cup of) coffee for you.

4. Please get me a (slice / piece / cup) of bread.

5. Do you want (some / a glass of / a bowl of) ice cream?

EXERCISE 6: Count and Non-Count Nouns: Verb Agreement

Write statements or questions. Use the words in parentheses and **is** or **are**. Remember to add the correct capitalization.

1. (apples / any / there / ?)

   Are there any apples? _____

2. (good / you / fruit / for / .)

   _____

3. (eggs / any / for breakfast / there / ?)

   _____

(continued on next page)

Count and Non-Count Nouns; *Some* and *Any* **103**

4. (delicious / the / candy / .)

_____

5. (the / at that restaurant / good / food / ?)

_____

6. (some / bread / there / .)

_____

7. (any / milk / there / ?)

_____

8. (salty / olives / these / .)

_____

EXERCISE 7: Count and Non-Count Nouns

Complete the sentences. Use **a, an, any,** _or_ **some.**

1. I don't have _____*any*_____ sisters or brothers.

2. I'm writing _____*an*_____ email message.

3. Do you have _____ questions?

4. I have _____ question.

5. I need _____ answer to this question.

6. I know _____ people from Canada.

7. I don't have _____ American friends.

8. We have _____ apartment on Main Street.

9. Is that _____ good restaurant?

10. We want _____ tea.

11. I don't want _____ candy.

12. Please give me _____ bananas.

EXERCISE 8: Editing

Correct the conversation. There are seven mistakes. The first mistake is already corrected. Find and correct six more.

JUDY: Excuse me, waiter? Can I have ~~some~~ *a* glass of water, please?

WAITER: Sure, ma'am. Do you want mineral or regular?

JUDY: Regular, please

[Minutes later]

WAITER: Here is your water. Are you ready to order?

JUDY: Yes. I'd like sandwich and a bowl of soup. Oh, and some small piece of chocolate cake too.

WAITER: And you, sir?

JOSH: Well, I'm not sure. Are the chicken here good?

WAITER: Yes, it's delicious.

JOSH: OK. I'd like any chicken. And bowl of ice cream.

WAITER: And what about something to drink?

JOSH: I want the water. Mineral water, please.

EXERCISE 9: Personal Writing

Write sentences about your usual breakfast, lunch, or dinner.

EXAMPLE: *For breakfast I usually have some orange juice. Then I have some cereal and milk. Sometimes I also have a piece of toast or a bagel. I never have eggs for breakfast.*

1. _____

2. _____

3. _____

4. _____

EXERCISE 1: Text Completion

Complete the conversation. Use the words from the box. Don't look at your Student Book.

~~a~~	any	formal	on	ones	size
an	fit	it	one	sale	the

CLERK: May I help you?

KEN: Yes, I'm looking for _____*a*_____ new

1.

sports jacket. I have _____

2.

interview tomorrow.

CLERK: Oh, you're in luck! We're having a

_____ on sports jackets.

3.

KEN: You are? Great!

CLERK: What _____?

4.

KEN: Forty-two.

CLERK: OK. Be right back.

CLERK: All right. Do you like _____ of

5.

these?

KEN: Yes! I really like _____ blue one.

6.

CLERK: Do you want to try it _____?

7.

KEN: Sure.

CLERK: How does it feel? Does it _____?
8.

KEN: Perfectly. And it's really comfortable. How does

_____ look, Laura?
9.

LAURA: Well, it's pretty bright. And it's casual. How

about that black _____? It's more
10.

_____.
11.

KEN: All the black _____ are dull—really boring.
12.

LAURA: OK. It's up to you.

Complete the sentences. Choose from the words in parentheses.

1. The shirt _____ isn't _____ on sale. The price is always $35.
   (is / isn't)

2. The shoes _____. They're small.
   (fit / don't fit

3. Men _____ formal jackets to an interview.
   (usually wear / don't usually wear)

4. Students _____ casual clothes to class.
   (often wear / don't often wear)

5. _____ is a bright color.
   (Yellow / Gray)

6. Those dark ties _____ dull. I like the red ones.
   (are / aren't)

7. People _____ try on shoes before they buy them.
   (usually / don't usually)

8. My shoes _____ a size 8.
   (are / aren't)

EXERCISE 3: *One / Ones*

Match the statements and questions with the responses.

__f__ 1. I like the blue umbrella.

____ 2. Here are your new suspenders.

____ 3. Do you like the stores on Main Street?

____ 4. I like the black pants.

____ 5. This is your new office.

____ 6. Do you go to the clothing store on Park Street?

a. No, I don't like that one.

b. No, I like the ones on First Street.

c. I like the brown ones.

d. I like the old one.

e. I want the old ones.

f. Really? I like the red one.

Look at the pictures. Answer the questions. Use **one** *or* **ones**.

1. Do you like the old car or the new car?

I like the <u>old one, OR *I like the new one*</u> .

2. Do you like the formal clothes or the casual clothes?

I like the _____.

3. Do you like the expensive earrings or the cheap earrings?

I like the _____.

4. Do you like the big car or the small car?

I like the _____.

5. Do you like the bright sweater or the dull sweater?

I like the _____.

EXERCISE 5: A / An and *The*

Look at the picture. Complete the conversation. Use **a, an,** *or* **the**.

A: What's in the picture?

B: I see _____*an*_____ apartment. I see _____ boy and
    1.   2.
_____ girl.
    3.

(continued on next page)

A: Where is _____ boy?
4.

B: He's sitting in _____ chair.
5.

A: Where is _____ girl?
6.

B: _____ girl is next to _____ window.
7.   8.

A: What is she doing?

B: She's watching _____ sun come up.
9.

A: What is _____ boy doing?
10.

B: He's eating _____ apple.
11.

EXERCISE 6: Article or No Article?

Complete the paragraphs. Use **a, an,** *or* **the.** *If no article is needed, write* **Ø.**

I shop at Clothes for You. It's _____*a*_____ nice store. It always has
1.

_____*Ø*_____ clothes in my size. It has _____ clothes for
2.   3.

_____ men and _____ women. _____ clothes there
4.   5.   6.

are alway nice and not very expensive.

I go to Nice Feet for _____ shoes. _____ shoes there are a little
7.   8.

expensive, but they're always comfortable. It's _____ big store, and it's usually
9.

busy. I know _____ clerk there. I don't know his name, but he's the only clerk
10.

there with _____ goatee. He also always wears _____ orange tie.
11.   12.

EXERCISE 7: Editing

Correct the conversations. There are eight mistakes. The first mistake is already corrected. Find and correct seven more.

1. **A:** Try on the green jacket.

                                       one
   B: But I prefer the brown.

2. **A:** Do you like the brown hat?

  B: No. I like the blue.

3. A: Do you wear your black slacks to school?

  B: No, I usually wear my gray one.

4. A: Do you wear the tie to work?

  B: No, I don't like the ties.

5. A: Do you have an white dress that I could try on?

  B: Yes, I do. Here's a small one and here's a large one.

6. A: Do you want a umbrella?

  B: No, I never use the umbrellas.

EXERCISE 8: Personal Writing

Write sentences about the clothes you like to wear.

EXAMPLE: *I usually wear casual clothes to school. I like to wear a T-shirt and jeans. They're very comfortable. My sports shoes are comfortable too.*

1. _____

2. _____

3. _____

4. _____

EXERCISE 1: Text Completion

Complete the conversation. Use the words from the box. Don't look at your Student Book.

an idea	Can someone	can't do	pronunciation	read	teach
can	can't	plan	Spanish	team	~~understand~~

JESSICA: What's the matter, Jeremy? You look really down.

JEREMY: I can't _____understand_____ my Spanish
      1.
teacher. She speaks too fast. And no

one _____ understand my
          2.
Spanish. My_____ is pretty
            3.
bad. I have to give a presentation Friday. I

_____ it.
      4.

JESSICA: But last year you were so good in _____.
                5.

JEREMY: It wasn't a conversation class. I can _____. I just can't speak.
                      6.

JESSICA: _____ in the class help?
        7.

JEREMY: No. I don't know anyone that well . . . But that gives me _____. You
                              8.
know Jorge, the star of our basketball _____?
                          9.

JESSICA: Uh-huh.

JEREMY: Well, Jorge's in my math class. He's not doing well. The coach says he has to pass

math or he _____ stay on the team.
          10.

JESSICA: Oh?

JEREMY: But he's fluent in Spanish. Maybe he can help me with Spanish and I can

_____ him math.
      11.

JESSICA: Well, that sounds like a _____.
                      12.

EXERCISE 2: Vocabulary

Complete the sentences. Use the words from the box.

~~coach~~	fluent	ideas	pass	star	team

1. The _____coach_____ worked with the players and helped them improve their game.

2. Margo is the best player on the team. She's the _____ of the team.

3. I study every night and _____ all my tests.

4. He lived in Mexico for many years. He's _____ in Spanish.

5. There are nine players on a baseball _____.

6. How can I improve my English? Do you have any _____?

EXERCISE 3: *Can*: Affirmative and Negative Statements

Complete the sentences. Use **can** *or* **can't**.

1. A bird _____can_____ fly.

2. A dog _____ fly.

3. A new baby _____ talk.

4. A fish _____ swim.

(continued on next page)

5. A cat _____ climb trees.

6. An elephant _____ climb trees.

7. A child _____ drive a car.

8. A bird _____ sing.

EXERCISE 4: *Can*: Affirmative and Negative Statements

Check (✔) the things you can do. Write sentences about what you can and can't do.

☐ **1.** pass an English test

I can pass an English test.

I'm studying beginning Chinese.

☐ **2.** speak fluent Chinese

I can't speak fluent Chinese.

☐ **3.** drive a car

_____

☐ **4.** park a car

_____

☐ **5.** lift weights at the gym

_____

☐ **6.** play chess

_____

☐ **7.** play on a basketball team

_____

☐ **8.** be a coach

_____

EXERCISE 5: *Can: Yes / No* Questions

Rewrite the requests. Use **can.**

1. Please do me a favor. <u>Can you do me a favor, please?</u>_____

2. Give Kathy this message, please. _____

3. Tell me the answers, please. _____

4. Call the babysitter, please. _____

5. Please wait for me. _____

6. Help me with my homework, please. _____

EXERCISE 6: *Can*: Affirmative and Negative Statements

Read the information in the chart. Then complete the sentences. Use **can** *or* **can't** *and the words in parentheses.*

Can they . . . ?	Amanda	Judy	Steve	Josh
Sing	yes	no	no	yes
Dance	yes	yes	no	no
Swim	yes	yes	yes	no
Play tennis	no	yes	no	no
Cook well	no	yes	no	no
Be a coach	no	yes	yes	yes
Play the guitar	yes	no	no	yes
Play chess	no	no	yes	yes

1. Amanda _____can sing_____ , and she _____can dance_____ .
                   (sing)   **(dance)**

2. Josh _____can sing_____ , but he _____can't dance_____ .
                  (sing)   **(dance)**

3. Steve and Josh _____ , but they _____ .
                         (dance)   **(play chess)**

4. Judy _____ , and she _____ .
                   (sing)   **(play the guitar)**

5. Judy _____ , and she _____ .
                   (play tennis)   **(cook well)**

6. Steve and Amanda _____ , but they
                         (swim)

   _____ .
           (play tennis)

7. Amanda _____ , and she _____ .
                   (cook well)   **(play chess)**

8. Amanda _____ , but she _____ .
                 (play the guitar)   **(be a coach)**

Now complete sentences about yourself.

9. I _____ , _____ I _____ .
             (sing)   **(dance)**

10. I _____ , _____ I _____ .
             (swim)   **(play tennis)**

EXERCISE 7: *Can: Yes / No* Questions

Write questions with **can**. *Then write short answers. Use the information in parentheses.*

1. **A:** _Can Blanca speak Spanish well?_

   B: _Yes, she can._ (Blanca can speak Spanish well.)

2. **A:** _____

   B: _____ (I can't speak French.)

3. **A:** _____

   B: _____ (Mike can't play the piano.)

4. **A:** _____

   B: _____ (Rosie can't understand Italian.)

5. **A:** _____

   B: _____ (The doctor can see you tomorrow.)

6. **A:** _____

   B: _____ (I can't go shopping with you today.)

EXERCISE 8: *Can: Wh-* Questions

Write questions. Use the words in parentheses and **can**. *Then write true short answers.*

1. (Where / I / get some coffee)

   Where can I get some coffee?   _At Hot Cup Café._

2. (How / I / learn your language)

   _____   _____

3. (Who / cut my hair)

   _____   _____

4. (Where / I / buy CDs)

   _____   _____

5. (What / I / do on the weekend in your town)

   _____   _____

EXERCISE 9: Editing

Correct the conversation. There are eight mistakes. The first mistake is already corrected. Find and correct seven more.

                                Can you

A: I have a problem. ~~You can~~ help me?

B: Sure. How do can I help?

A: I can't not understand the homework. Can you understand it?

B: Yes, I do. But I can't to explain it well. Cans the teacher explain it to you?

A: I can't to find him.

B: He's in his office. I'm sure he can helps you.

EXERCISE 10: Personal Writing

Write sentences about what you and people in your family **can** *or* **can't** *do.*

EXAMPLE: *I can play the piano. My brother can play the guitar, but he can't play the piano.*

1. _____

2. _____

3. _____

4. _____

UNIT 22 Simple Past: Regular Verbs (Statements)

EXERCISE 1: Text Completion

Complete the emails. Use the words from the box. Don't look at your Student Book.

apartment	checked out	didn't finish	ended	looked	party
arrived	convention	~~enjoyed~~	I'm staying	missed	

Kathy,

Thanks for the delicious chocolates. Everyone at the party _____*enjoyed*_____
1.
them. The party was a blast, but we all _____ you, especially Mark.
2.
He _____ very lonely. :>(
3.
How's Boston? How's the _____?
4.
Judy

Judy,

Once again, happy birthday!

Boston is terrific :)! But the convention was a lot of work.

I _____ here late Monday night. Tuesday I worked from 7:00 in the
5.
morning until 10:00 at night. Wednesday I started at 7:00 and _____
6.
until 9:00 at night. The convention finally _____ last night.
7.

(continued on next page)

This morning I _____ of my hotel. _____ with my
                        8.   9.

cousin Ted for a couple of days. He's a really nice guy, and he has a great

_____. I'd like you to meet him.
        10.

Again, I'm so sorry I missed your _____.
                                            11.

Kathy

Hi Kathy,

_____ this cousin? I'd love to meet him.
        12.

Judy

EXERCISE 2: Vocabulary

Read the sentences. Write **T (True)** *or* **F (False).**

_____ 1. I stayed home last night.

_____ 2. I didn't miss class two weeks ago.

_____ 3. The teacher arrived late to class last week.

_____ 4. I attended a convention last month.

_____ 5. I checked into a hotel last year.

_____ 6. Class didn't end early last week.

_____ 7. I didn't check out of a hotel yesterday.

_____ 8. I didn't enjoy class last week.

EXERCISE 3: Simple Past: Affirmative Statements

*Complete the sentences. Use the simple past of the verbs from the box. Put a check (✔)
next to the things you did last night.*

check in	listen	play	~~talk~~	visit	watch

_____ 1. I ___talked___ on the phone.   _____ 4. I _____ at the Grand Hotel.

_____ 2. I _____ TV all night.   _____ 5. I _____ my grandparents.

_____ 3. I _____ to the radio.   _____ 6. I _____ computer games.

EXERCISE 4: Simple Past: Affirmative and Negative Statements

Complete the sentences. Use the simple past.

1. I cook dinner at 6:00 every evening.

   I _____cooked_____ dinner at 6:00 yesterday evening.

2. I don't clean on Mondays.

   I _____didn't clean_____ last Monday.

3. Anton arrives on time every day.

   Anton _____ on time yesterday.

4. Tim doesn't cook.

   He _____ last night.

5. Steve enjoys his class.

   He _____ his class last week.

6. Yuko and Omar study at the library every morning.

   They _____ at the library yesterday morning.

7. We call our children every weekend.

   We _____ our children last weekend.

8. The students ask a lot of questions in every class.

   They _____ a lot of questions in class today.

9. We don't want to go to the movies late at night.

   We _____ to go to the movies late last night.

10. I don't buy shoes from that store.

    I _____ these shoes from that store.

EXERCISE 5: Past Time Expressions

Complete the sentences. Use **yesterday, ago,** *or* **last.**

1. I watched a good movie _____last_____ night.

2. Maya missed class two days _____.

3. Juan wasn't late for class _____ morning.

(continued on next page)

4. Diego arrived in the United States _____ summer.

5. Claire visited Spain one week _____.

6. The presentation we attended _____ was interesting.

7. The convention started _____ Friday.

8. We called my grandparents _____ afternoon.

9. The weather wasn't so cold a month _____.

10. My friends and I studied until late _____ night.

EXERCISE 6: Simple Past: Negative Statements

Complete the sentences. Use the negative simple past of the verb.

1. I visited my parents, but I _____*didn't visit*_____ my grandparents.

2. I watched TV, but I _____ a DVD.

3. She talked to her brother, but she _____ to her sister.

4. They enjoyed the movie, but they _____ the book.

5. We played golf, but we _____ chess.

6. He learned French, but he _____ Spanish.

EXERCISE 7: Editing

Correct the email message. There are six mistakes. The first mistake is already corrected. Find and correct five more.

Subj: Rita Jonas
Date: September 7   9:52 P.M.
From: h.Okun@adsu.com
   To: t.Olson@adsu.com

Thanks for dinner last week. I ~~enjoy~~ *enjoyed* it very much. I hope I not talk too much. I

was liked your kids a lot. Jeremy did show me some great computer games.

I talked to Rita's secretary again yesterday, but Rita didn't returned my call.

Herb

P.S. Sorry I didn't thanked you before, but I was very busy.

EXERCISE 8: Personal Writing

Write four affirmative and four negative sentences about last weekend. Use the verbs in Unit 22 of the Student Book.

EXAMPLE: *Saturday it rained. I stayed home. I didn't work in the garden.*

1. _____
2. _____
3. _____
4. _____
5. _____
6. _____
7. _____
8. _____

Simple Past: Regular and Irregular Verbs; *Yes / No* Questions

Complete the conversation. Use the words from the box. Don't look at your Student Book.

acted	began	didn't have	I did	moved	was born
actor	Did	happened	made	was	~~wrote~~

JEREMY: Dad? I _____*wrote*_____ this paper for my drama

    1.

class. Can you read what I have so far?

TIM: Sure, Jeremy. What's the assignment?

JEREMY: We have to write about an _____ we

    2.

admire. I picked Christopher Reeve.

    Christopher Reeve, An Admirable Actor

    Christopher Reeve _____

        3.

on September 25, 1952, in New York City. He

_____ to act at the age of nine when he

    4.

got a part in his first play. He _____ in a

        5.

lot of plays during his teenage years and many more

when he went to Cornell University. After college he

_____ to New York City and worked in

    6.

theater.

    Christopher had his first role in a Hollywood

movie in 1978. Today he is most famous as

the star of the *Superman* movies. Christopher

_____ four *Superman* films.

    7.

    A sad thing _____ to Christopher

        8.

on May 27, 1995. He was in a horseback riding

competition and fell off his horse. He _____ paralyzed below his
9.
neck and had to spend the rest of his life in a wheelchair. But he didn't give up.

He started an organization to help people who are paralyzed. His organization

gave a lot of money for research.

In 2004, Christopher Reeve died of a heart attack. He _____ a
10.
long life, but he did a lot of good things. We will remember him for a long time.

TIM: This is really good, Jeremy. _____ you use the Internet to get your
11.
information?

JEREMY: Yes, _____.
12.

TIM: Well, I think people will like your paper.

EXERCISE 2: Vocabulary

Complete the chart. Write the base form of the verb. Check (✔) **Regular Verb** *or*
Irregular Verb.

		Base Form of Verb	Regular Verb	Irregular Verb
1.	I <u>got</u> a book at the library last week.	*get*		✔
2.	I <u>picked</u> an interesting book.	*pick*	✔	
3.	The writer <u>was born</u> in China.			
4.	He <u>acted</u> in a lot of plays in China.			
5.	He <u>moved</u> to France with his wife.			
6.	He <u>gave up</u> acting.			
7.	He <u>wrote</u> plays in Chinese and French.			
8.	He <u>became</u> very rich.			
9.	He <u>gave</u> a lot of money to Chinese writers.			
10.	One day he <u>fell</u> off his bike.			
11.	The fall badly <u>injured</u> him.			
12.	He <u>died later</u> in France.			

EXERCISE 3: Simple Past: Irregular Verbs; Affirmative and Negative Statements

Complete the sentences about yourself. Use the affirmative or negative simple past forms of the verbs in parentheses.

1. I _____*had*_____ dinner late yesterday.
     (have)

2. I _____ a test last week.
     (take)

3. I _____ well last night.
     (sleep)

4. My teacher _____ to my home last weekend.
     (come)

5. A friend _____ me a gift two days ago.
     (get)

6. My family _____ on vacation last month.
     (go)

7. I _____ a new book last week.
     (begin)

8. One of my classmates _____ in the cafeteria this morning.
     (fall)

EXERCISE 4: Simple Past: Irregular Verbs; Affirmative and Negative Statements

Change the sentences to the simple past. Write about the day in parentheses.

1. I have breakfast every morning.

   (today) _*I had breakfast today.*_____

2. Sarah eats lunch every day.

   (today) _____

3. Matthew gets up early every morning.

   (today) _____

4. Yoshi sleeps eight hours every night.

   (last night) _____

5. Jay and Diego go to the library every day.

   (yesterday) _____

6. Jennifer Lopez makes a movie every year.

   (last year) _____

EXERCISE 5: Simple Past: Irregular Verbs; Negative Statements

Change the sentences to the simple past.

1. Makiko doesn't do her homework. _Makiko didn't do her homework._

2. Henry doesn't go to bed at 8:00. _____

3. Maria doesn't eat breakfast at school. _____

4. John and Mary don't make lunch at home. _____

5. Linda doesn't see her friends at school. _____

EXERCISE 6: Simple Past: *Yes / No* Questions and Short Answers

*Write **yes** / **no** questions. Then write short answers. Use the information in parentheses.*

1. **A:** _Did you go to bed late yesterday?_

   B: _Yes, I did._ _____ (I went to bed late yesterday.)

2. **A:** _____

   B: _____ (The teacher drank coffee in class last

   week.)

3. **A:** _____

   B: _____ (My friends and I didn't go to a party last

   week.)

4. **A:** _____

   B: _____ (Robert didn't drink coffee today.)

5. **A:** _____

   B: _____ (Ann and Jeffrey fell off their bicycles today.)

6. **A:** _____

   B: _____ (My friends didn't come to my home last

   week.)

7. **A:** _____

   B: _____ (My friends gave me money today.)

EXERCISE 7: Editing

Correct the conversations. There are seven mistakes. The first mistake is already corrected. Find and correct six more.

1. **A:** ~~You did~~ *Did you* sleep well last night?

   B: No, I wasn't.

2. **A:** I go to a party last Saturday.

   B: Did you have fun?

3. **A:** Did you eat anything last night?

   B: No, and I not drink anything either.

4. **A:** I didn't saw my keys on the table.

   B: We gived them to your roommate.

5. **A:** Did you went to school yesterday?

   B: Yes, I went to school.

EXERCISE 8: Personal Writing

Write sentences about a grandparent. Use irregular simple past verbs where possible.

EXAMPLE: *My grandmother was born in 1932. She married my grandfather, and they came to the United States in 1952.*

1. _____

2. _____

3. _____

4. _____

UNIT 24 Simple Past: *Wh-* Questions

EXERCISE 1: Text Completion

Complete the conversations. Use the words from the box. Don't look at your Student Book.

accident	did	do	happened	took	What
car	didn't want	happen	How	was	~~When~~

AMANDA: Hi, Rob. What's up? . . . Are you OK? . . . Well, that's

good. ____When____ did it happen? . . . Where did
　　　　　　1.

it _____? . . . Are you there now? . . . Why
　　　　2.

_____ you *drive*? . . . Does Dad know?
　　3.

[Amanda hangs up.]

JOSH: What _____?
　　　　　　4.

AMANDA: Rob had a car _____ this morning.
　　　　　　　　　　　　5.

JOSH: How is he?

AMANDA: He's fine, but the car is damaged. He _____
　　　　　　　　　　　　　　　　　　　　　　6.

to walk to the supermarket in the rain, so he

_____ Dad's car.
　　7.

JOSH: _____ happened to the car?
　　　　　8.

AMANDA: One of the headlights is broken, and there's a big

dent in the bumper.

JOSH: _____ did it happen?
　　　　　9.

AMANDA: I guess the road _____ slippery. The car
　　　　　　　　　　　　　　10.

skidded on some leaves and hit a pole.

JOSH: That's too bad.

AMANDA: And Rob drove Dad's _____ without his OK.
　　　　　　　　　　　　　　　　11.

JOSH: Uh-oh.

(continued on next page)

AMANDA: He's at Charlie's Auto Repair Shop now. It will cost $600 to fix the car.

JOSH: Six hundred dollars? Poor Dad.

AMANDA: What _____ you mean "poor Dad"? Poor
             12.
Rob.

EXERCISE 2: Vocabulary

Match the words and definitions.

   _c_ **1.** an accident

  _____ **2.** an auto repair shop

  _____ **3.** a bumper

  _____ **4.** a dent

  _____ **5.** headlights

  _____ **6.** slippery

a. You see this at the front and back of a car. It protects the car.

b. You see these at the front of a car. They help the driver see at night.

c. This is something bad that happens. People don't plan it.

d. Roads are often like this after it rains or snows.

e. This is something you often see on a car after another car hits it.

f. This is a place that fixes cars.

EXERCISE 3: Simple Past: *Wh-* Questions

Match the questions and answers.

  _d_ **1.** What time did you get up?

  _____ **2.** What did you have for breakfast?

  _____ **3.** Who made breakfast for you?

  _____ **4.** What did you do after breakfast?

  _____ **5.** How did you get there?

  _____ **6.** Where did you have lunch?

a. A bagel and fruit.

b. At the beach.

c. We took the bus.

d. At 7:30.

e. My mother.

f. We went to the beach.

EXERCISE 4: Simple Past: *Wh-* Questions

*Circle the correct **Wh-** word to complete each question.*

1. Who / **When** did you go for a drive?

2. Where / **What** did you go?

3. Who / **Why** went with you?

4. What / **What time** did you leave?

5. Why / **Who** did you go for a drive?

6. When / **What** happened on your trip?

Read the story about an accident. Complete the questions in the conversation with
what, when, where, *or* **who.** *Use the information in the answers to help you.*

     The accident happened at First and Main at 8:02. The driver of a black BMW didn't stop at a red light. The driver of a white Toyota didn't see the BMW. The driver of the Toyota hit the BMW. The drivers got out of their cars. They had a fight. Two men on the street stopped the fight. A woman saw the accident and called the police. They came to the accident quickly.

1. A: _____*Where*_____ did the accident happen?

    B: At First and Main.

2. A: _____ did the accident happen?

    B: At 8:02.

3. A: _____ did the driver of the BMW do?

    B: He didn't stop at a red light.

4. A: _____ hit the BMW?

    B: The driver of a white Toyota.

5. A: _____ got out of their cars?

    B: Both drivers got out of their cars.

6. A: _____ happened?

    B: The drivers had a fight.

(continued on next page)

7. A: _____ stopped the fight?

   B: Two men on the street.

8. A: _____ did the woman do?

   B: She called the police.

EXERCISE 6: Simple Past: Statements and Questions

Complete the conversation. Use the simple past of the words in parentheses. Use **did** *in questions where necessary.*

AMANDA: _____ *I called* _____ you on the weekend, but _____ home.
               1. (I / call)   2. (you / not be)

        Where _____?
                  3. (you / go)

KATHY: _____ to Mark's parents' house.
           4. (we / go)

AMANDA: Oh? _____ there all weekend?
               5. (you / stay)

KATHY: Yes. _____ two nights there. _____ there on Friday
             6. (we / spend)   7. (we / drive)

      night, and _____ back last night.
                  8. (we / get)

AMANDA: What _____ there?
            9. (you / do)

KATHY: Well, on Saturday morning _____ home with Mark's parents and
                         10. (we / stay)

      _____.
          11. (talk)

AMANDA: What _____ about?
            12. (you / talk)

KATHY: Lots of different things. _____ about funny things
                   13. (I / learn)

      _____ as a child and about other people in his family.
          14. (Mark / do)

AMANDA: _____ anybody else in the family?
         15. (you / meet)

KATHY: Yeah. In the evening, _____ a party for us.
                 16. (they / have)

AMANDA: Who _____?
         17. (come)

KATHY: A lot of people—aunts, uncles, and cousins.

AMANDA: So _____ the whole family?
         18. (you / meet)

KATHY: Just about.

AMANDA: _____ fun?
        19. (it / be)

KATHY: Oh, yeah. _____ myself a lot.
        20. (I / enjoy)

EXERCISE 7: Editing

Correct the conversations. There are nine mistakes. The first mistake is already corrected. Find and correct eight more.

                  did you drive

1. **A:** Why ~~drove you~~ your parents' car yesterday?

   B: My car was at the auto repair shop.

2. **A:** Who did fix the car?

   B: The mechanic fix it yesterday.

3. **A:** Why did you took your car to the auto repair shop?

   B: Because a truck hitted my car and I had a big dent in the bumper.

4. **A:** Why did your mother was angry with you?

   B: I drive her car without her OK.

5. **A:** What time the accident happened?

   B: It happened at 2:30.

6. **A:** How the roads were?

   B: They were slippery.

EXERCISE 8: Personal Writing

Think about a recent news story—for example, an accident or a fire. Imagine you are a news reporter. Write questions to ask. Use **how, how long, what, when, where, who,** *or* **why.**

EXAMPLE: *How did the fire start?*

1. _____

2. _____

3. _____

4. _____

UNIT 25 **Subject and Object Pronouns**

EXERCISE 1: Text Completion

Complete the conversation. Use the words from the box. Don't look at your Student Book.

flowers	He	him	me	to	you
~~gift~~	her	I	them	us	your

CARLOS: Kathy, you're an American. What's a good _____*gift*_____?
1.

KATHY: For what?

CARLOS: For the party at Bill's house on Saturday. I want to get _____ a gift.
2.

KATHY: Right. Let me think.

CARLOS: How about _____?
3.

KATHY: Well, I suppose so. But you don't usually give flowers _____ a man.
4.

CARLOS: _____ has a wife. Can I give them to _____?
5. 6.

KATHY: Hmm. I'm not sure.

CARLOS: What about tickets for a concert? I know he likes music.

KATHY: No. Not appropriate. You don't give _____ boss tickets.
7.

134

CARLOS: Well, what do you suggest?

KATHY: Why don't you give him some chocolates? He's always eating _____ at his
8.
desk.

CARLOS: OK, good idea. A box of chocolates. Now, can you do me a favor?

KATHY: What?

CARLOS: Tomiko and _____ need a ride to the party. Can you take _____?
9.   10.

KATHY: For a price.

CARLOS: For a price? What do you mean?

KATHY: Get _____ a box of chocolates too.
11.

CARLOS: I don't believe you. You're not serious, are you?

KATHY: No, just kidding! I'll pick _____ up at 6:30 on Saturday.
12.

EXERCISE 2: Vocabulary

*Match the words and the gifts. Then say who the gifts are good for. Write the names of
family members or friends.*

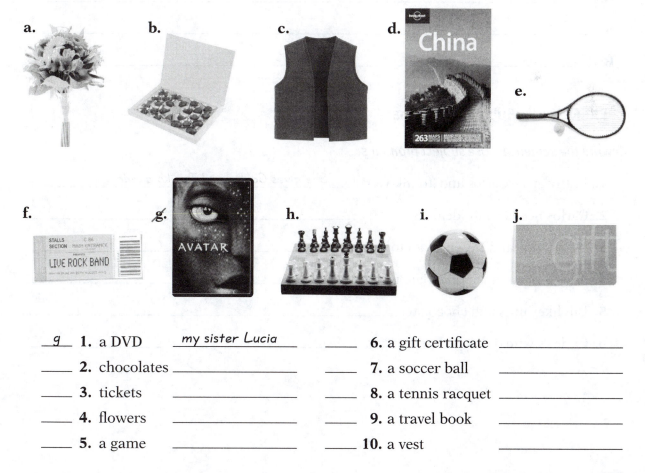

a.   b.   c.   d. China   e.

f. LIVE ROCK BAND   g. AVATAR   h.   i.   j.

__g__ 1. a DVD   *my sister Lucia*   ____ 6. a gift certificate _____

____ 2. chocolates _____   ____ 7. a soccer ball   _____

____ 3. tickets   _____   ____ 8. a tennis racquet _____

____ 4. flowers   _____   ____ 9. a travel book   _____

____ 5. a game   _____   ____ 10. a vest   _____

EXERCISE 3: Subject and Object Pronouns

Write a conversation. Use the sentences from the box.

> How about a tennis racquet?
>
> Hmm. What does she like?
>
> Then why don't you get her a gift certificate?
>
> Happy to help you.
>
> They are too expensive.
>
> ~~It's my friend's birthday tomorrow. What's a good gift for her?~~
>
> That's a good idea. I'll get her a gift certificate at a sporting goods store! Thanks!
>
> Well, she likes sports.

A: *It's my friend's birthday tomorrow. What's a good gift for her?*

B: _____

A: _____

B: _____

A: _____

B: _____

A: _____

B: _____

EXERCISE 4: Subject Pronouns

Rewrite the sentences. Use subject pronouns.

1. Kathy gives Carlos and Tomiko a ride. *She gives Carlos and Tomiko a ride.*

2. Carlos needs a gift idea. _____

3. My friends and I want to go to the party. _____

4. A DVD is not an appropriate gift. _____

5. Bill likes nuts and chocolate. _____

6. Carlos's wife didn't go to the party. _____

EXERCISE 5: Object Pronouns

Rewrite the sentences. Use object pronouns.

1. I didn't see Carlos. _I didn't see him._

2. Kathy drove the car to the party. _____

3. I talked to Bill and Carlos. _____

4. I didn't see you and Tomiko. _____

5. Bill loves chocolate. _____

6. Bill talked to me and my friend. _____

EXERCISE 6: Object Pronouns

Complete the conversations. Use **me, you, him, her, it, us,** *or* **them.**

1. **A:** Here, Bill. This gift is for _____*you*_____.

   B: Thanks a lot.

2. **A:** Is this gift appropriate for Bill?

   B: Yes, I think it's OK to give _____ chocolates.

3. **A:** How did you get here? Did Sandra give _____ a ride?

   B: No. Kathy brought _____.

4. **A:** You walked all the way here? You're kidding! I don't believe _____.

   B: It's true. Walking is nice. I love _____.

5. **A:** Carlos, can I use your cell phone?

   B: I don't have _____ here.

6. **A:** Does Carlos know your wife?

   B: Yes. He's talking to _____ right now.

7. **A:** Tomiko, do you like these earrings?

   B: Yes, I like _____ very much.

8. **A:** You and your girlfriend didn't come to the party.

   B: That's because nobody invited _____.

Complete the conversations with subject and object pronouns.

1. **A:** Where are the chips?

   B: _____They_____ are in the dining room. I put _____them_____ on the table.

2. **A:** Did you invite Carlos and Tomiko? I like _____.

   B: Yes, _____ are coming with Kathy. _____ has a car.

3. **A:** Did you invite Mark?

   B: I invited _____, but _____ can't come.

4. **A:** This chair is heavy. I can't move _____. Can you help _____?

   B: Sure.

5. **A:** Oh, somebody's at the door. Can you open _____?

   B: _____'s already open.

6. **A:** Hello, Tomiko. It's nice to meet _____. Bill talks about _____ all

   the time.

   B: Really? Does _____ say nice things?

7. **A:** Bill, Tomiko is thirsty. Can you bring _____ a soda, please?

   B: But _____ is drinking some soda right now.

8. **A:** Bill, there are chocolates on the table. Are they for _____?

   B: Yes, Carlos bought _____ for you and me.

EXERCISE 8: Editing

Correct the note. There are eight mistakes. The first mistake is already corrected. Find and correct seven more.

Dear Anne,

    Thank you for inviting ~~we~~ us to the party. The children and me had a great time. The games were great. The kids loved they.

    Did Bob and Sally find the gifts? I left it in their rooms. Did Bob like the tennis racquet? I bought it at Central Sports for he. I got Sally's soccer ball there too. Does her still play soccer? (I know you said "No gifts," but what's a birthday without gifts?)

    Why don't us meet one day for lunch? Give I a call.

Talk to you soon,

Sarah

EXERCISE 9: Personal Writing

Write a thank-you note for a gift you received. Use subject and object pronouns.

EXAMPLE: Dear Aunt Emma and Uncle Henry,

Thank you very much for the earrings. I love them. They're really beautiful. I'm wearing them right now. You are so good to me!

Thanks again.

Love,
Lucia

_____

_____

_____

_____

_____

_____

UNIT 26 — How much / How many; Quantity Expressions

EXERCISE 1: Text Completion

Complete the conversation. Use the words from the box. Don't look at your Student Book.

ate	expensive	How many	much	That	was
did	~~how~~	hundreds	people	time	were

STEVE: So _____ *how* _____ was Ecuador?
   1.

JESSICA: Great.

STEVE: _____ days were you away?
   2.

JESSICA: Ten. We _____ in the capital,
   3.

Quito, and on the Galápagos Islands.

MARK: The Galápagos Islands? _____ sounds exciting. How much
   4.

_____ did you spend there?
   5.

TIM: Not _____. Only four days. But it _____ fantastic.
   6.   **7.**

We took _____ of photos of the plants and animals. We
   8.

_____ and slept on a boat.
   9.

MARK: Really? How many _____ were on the boat?
   10.

JESSICA: Twelve including us.

STEVE: How much _____ the trip cost?
   11.

JESSICA: It was _____, but we used our frequent flier miles for the flight.
   12.

MARK: Well, nothing beats travel.

TIM: I agree.

EXERCISE 2: Vocabulary

Complete the sentences. Write the correct forms of the words from the box.

animal	flight	only
capital	island	plant

1. The children love to go to the zoo to see the ____animals____.

2. Quito is the _____ of Ecuador.

3. The _____ took over 12 hours. It was a long trip!

4. England and Japan are both countries that are _____.

5. She has many beautiful flowers and other _____ in her garden.

6. We spent _____ four days there, but it was fantastic!

EXERCISE 3: *How much / How many*

Answer the questions about your last vacation. Use a number or choose from the short answers from the box.

A lot.	None.	Not many.	Not much.

1. How many days were you away? _A lot._ OR _Not many._

2. How much did the flight cost? _____

3. How many islands did you visit? _____

4. How many photos of plants did you take? _____

5. How many other tourists were with you? _____

6. How much sightseeing did you do? _____

7. How many expensive meals did you have? _____

8. How much time were you alone? _____

9. How many unusual animals did you see? _____

10. How much time did you spend in the capital? _____

EXERCISE 4: *How much / How many*

Write a conversation. Use the sentences from the box.

> Just a little, because the food wasn't great. But the prices were good.
>
> ~~How was the restaurant?~~
>
> How many people were there?
>
> Not much—only $30 for all of us.
>
> It was OK.
>
> How much did you eat?
>
> Four of us.
>
> Really? How much did you spend?

A: ___How was the restaurant?___

B: _____

A: _____

B: _____

A: _____

B: _____

A: _____

B: _____

EXERCISE 5: General Quantity Expressions

Circle the letter of the best answer.

1. How many workers does the hotel have?

   a. A lot.   **b.** Not much.   **c.** A little.

2. How many parking spaces does the hotel have?

   a. Much.   **b.** Not much.   **c.** Not many.

3. How many rooms does the hotel have?

   a. Much.   **b.** A lot.   **c.** A little.

4. How much money does it cost to stay at the hotel?

   a. A few.   **b.** Many.   **c.** Not much.

5. How many days did you stay there?

   a. Much.   **b.** Not much.   **c.** A few.

6. How much furniture do the rooms have?

   a. Many.   **b.** Not much.   **c.** A few.

7. How many meals do people eat at the hotel?

   a. Not many.   **b.** Not much.   **c.** Much.

8. How much time do people spend in the swimming pool?

   a. A few.   **b.** Many.   **c.** A lot.

EXERCISE 6: *How much / How many*

*Look at the picture of Steve's refrigerator. Write questions. Use **how many** or **how much** and the words in parentheses. Then write answers. Use **a lot, not many,** or **not much.***

1. (potatoes)

   How many potatoes does Steve have? _____   A lot. _____

2. (oranges)

   _____   _____

(continued on next page)

3. (bananas)

_____   _____

4. (milk)

_____   _____

5. (apples)

_____   _____

6. (soda)

_____   _____

7. (yogurt)

_____   _____

8. (juice)

_____   _____

9. (eggs)

_____   _____

10. (food)

_____   _____

EXERCISE 7: Editing

Correct the conversation. There are six mistakes. The first mistake is already corrected.
Find and correct five more.

         much

A: How ~~many~~ time do you get for vacation?

B: Four weeks.

A: Do you spend lot of time at home during your vacation?

B: No, only a little days.

A: Where do you usually go?

B: We spend a few time at my wife's parents' home. Then we go to the beach. We spend

    some time with our friends there.

A: How many friend do you see at the beach?

B: Not much. Four or five.

EXERCISE 8: Personal Writing

Write questions to ask a friend who was on vacation. Use **how much** *and* **how many** *in your questions.*

EXAMPLE: *How many days were you on vacation? How much sightseeing did you do?*

1. _____

2. _____

3. _____

4. _____

EXERCISE 1: Text Completion

Complete the conversation. Use the words from the box. Don't look at your Student Book.

a	is there	a lot of	they
are	It	there's	~~vacation~~
is	it's	there	went

JUDY: OK. So where did you guys go on your

_____vacation_____?
       1.

JOSH: South Dakota. We _____ there
                 2.

especially to see Mount Rushmore.

ELENA: There's something famous about Mount

Rushmore, isn't there?

AMANDA: Yes, there _____. There
                  3.

_____ four presidents' heads
     4.

carved into the mountain. Here's a picture of

them.

JOSH: Do you know who _____ are?
                   5.

JUDY: Sure. Washington, Jefferson, Theodore

Roosevelt, and Lincoln.

ELENA: Wow! _____ looks like a
               6.

fantastic place. What else _____
                            7.

to see in the area?

JOSH: Well, there's _____ great
8.

national park called The Badlands. It's only

about 60 miles away, and _____
9.

beautiful.

AMANDA: And _____ are two
10.

interesting old mining towns called Lead

and Deadwood.

JOSH: And there are _____ caves in
11.

the area.

AMANDA: And _____ a little town called
12.

Wall. It has an amazing drugstore—maybe

the biggest one in the world.

JUDY: Do you want to go back next year? Elena

and I will go with you. Show us more.

EXERCISE 2: Vocabulary

Complete the sentences with the names of streets in your city or places in your country.

1. There's usually a traffic jam on _____*Water*_____ Street.

2. There are caves in _____*South Dakota*_____.

3. There's a drugstore on _____ Street.

4. There's a waterfall in _____.

5. There's a bed-and-breakfast on _____ Street.

6. There's a famous monument in _____.

7. There's a national park in _____.

8. There's a snack bar on _____ Street.

9. There's a statue on _____ Street.

10. There's an amusement park in _____.

EXERCISE 3: *There is / There are:* Affirmative and Negative Statements

Look at the picture. Complete the sentences. Use **'s, isn't** *(or* **'s not**)*,* **are,** *or* **aren't.**

1. There *'s* _____ a window with a
   view.

2. There ____*isn't*____ a TV in the
   room.

3. There _____ cups on the
   table.

4. There _____ any glasses on
   the table.

5. There _____ a sink in the
   room.

6. There _____ a radio in the
   room.

7. There _____ any books in
   the room.

8. There _____ towels in the
   room.

9. There _____ a suitcase on
   the bed.

10. There _____ some pictures
    on the walls.

11. There _____ a desk in the
    room.

12. There _____ a mirror above
    the sink.

EXERCISE 4: *There is / There are:* Affirmative and Negative Statements

Write sentences about your neighborhood. Use **there** *and the words in parentheses.*

1. (apartment building) *There aren't many apartment buildings in my neighborhood.*

2. (supermarket) *There is a supermarket in my neighborhood.*

3. (drugstore) _____

4. (post office) _____

5. (library) _____

6. (stores) _____

7. (park) _____

8. (bank) _____

9. (movie theaters) _____

10. (restaurants) _____

EXERCISE 5: *Is there / Are there:* Questions

Put the words in the correct order. Write questions. Remember to add the correct capitalization.

1. station / nearby / a / is / there / subway / ?

   Is there a subway station nearby?

2. block / any / are / on / banks / there / this / ?

   _____

3. near / is / drugstore / a / here / there / ?

   _____

4. in / area / any / there / this / are / theaters / ?

   _____

5. many / area / monuments / are / in / how / this / there / ?

   _____

6. the / is / mall / there / elevator / in / an / ?

   _____

(continued on next page)

7. national park / are / in / any / restaurants / there / the / good / ?

_____

8. there / here / amusement park / around / is / an / ?

_____

EXERCISE 6: *There is / There are:* **Questions and Answers**

Complete the conversation. Use **there** *with* **is, are, isn't,** *or* **aren't.**

A: South Park is a good place to go.

B: <u> Are there </u> interesting things to do there?
        1.

A: Yes, _____.
        2.

B: _____ bed-and-breakfasts to stay at?
    3.

A: No, _____ many. But it's fun to visit.
       4.

B: _____ a snack bar to eat at?
    5.

A: Yes, _____.
        6.

B: _____ a tour we can take?
    7.

A: No, _____. Not today.
       8.

B: _____ an art museum we can visit?
    9.

A: Yes, _____. It's close to the train station.
       10.

B: _____ a place where I can send an email?
    11.

A: _____. You can use the computer at the library.
    12.

EXERCISE 7: Editing

Correct the email message. There are seven mistakes. The first mistake is already corrected. Find and correct six more.

Subj: Hello from Prague!
Date: Wednesday, June 3
From: akang@jahoo.com
   To: r.hudson@adsu.edu

Hi, Rob!

Greetings from Prague! We are having a great time here. Our hotel is very nice;
~~there's~~ *it's* a clean, comfortable place. It's close to everything we want to see.

There's many things to see and do here. They is a fantastic museum not very far from

our room. We went to Old Town today. It's an unusual clock there. It is so interesting!

They are also some beautiful statues there.

Let's see . . . are there anything else? Oh, yes! We saw a very beautiful, old bridge

yesterday. On the other side, it was a castle! It's so amazing to be here. This place has

a long, rich history.

I have to go now. We're going to see a movie tonight. Say hi to everyone for me.

Love,

Alison

EXERCISE 8: Personal Writing

Write sentences about the good things your neighborhood. Use **there is, there are, it is,**
and **they are.**

EXAMPLE: *My neighborhood is quiet. There isn't a lot of noise.*

1. _____

2. _____

3. _____

4. _____

PART X

MODIFIERS; COMPARISONS; PREPOSITIONS OF TIME

UNIT 28

Noun and Adjective Modifiers

EXERCISE 1: Text Completion

Complete the personal ads. Use the words from the box. Don't look at your Student Book.

a	chemistry	~~fun-loving~~	modern	similar	walks
an	fast	major	old	spy	woman

The Seattle Daily

♥ ♥ ♥ ♥ *Love Lines* ♥ ♥ ♥ ♥

MEN

Am I for you? Are you interested in a 35-year-old, *fun-loving* man? I enjoy jazz bands and sandy
1.

beaches. I'm looking for _____ kind, sensitive woman.
2.

I'm a rich, healthy, active 80-year-_____ man. I love to travel to beautiful places. I want to enjoy
3.

life with a lively middle-aged _____.
4.

I'm a 25-year-old _____ professor. I enjoy bird-watching and long _____ in the
5. 6.

country. I'm looking for a woman with similar interests.

WOMEN

Let's get together. I'm _____ artistic 20-year-old woman. I like modern art and
7.

_____ dance.
8.

I'm a tall 19-year-old college woman. I'm a computer science _____. I like computers, tennis,
9.

mystery movies, and _____ cars. I'm looking for a smart guy with similar interests.
10.

75-year-old woman. Rich, funny, warm, and honest. Enjoys _____ movies and travel to unusual
11.

places. Looking for a younger man with _____ interests.
12.

EXERCISE 2: Vocabulary

Complete the sentences. Use the words from the box.

artistic woman	computer science major	honest man	spy movies
~~chemistry professor~~	fun-loving man	personal ads	

1. My ___chemistry professor___ is an excellent teacher. He helped me understand this difficult subject.

2. My father is a very _____. He always tells the truth.

3. Many people answer _____. My best friend met her husband that way!

4. Her sister paints, draws, and makes her own clothes. She's a very _____.

5. I'm a _____. It's an excellent field with many wonderful job opportunities.

6. He is always having fun and laughing. He's a _____.

7. We love _____ because they're full of action and adventure.

EXERCISE 3: Sentences with Adjective + Noun

Complete the sentences. Use any adjectives that make sense.

1. I had ___Italian___ food for dinner last night.

2. _____ cities are fun to visit.

3. _____ people make me angry.

4. I have a(n) _____ family.

5. Yesterday was a(n) _____ day.

6. I think _____ people are interesting.

7. China is a(n) _____ country.

8. I am a(n) _____ person.

EXERCISE 4: Adjective Modifiers

Combine the sentences.

1. He is an older man. He is fun-loving.

   He is a fun-loving, older man.

2. Venus and Serena Williams are athletes. They are famous.

3. Jessica and Tim live in a house. The house is big.

4. Josh and Amanda ate at a restaurant. The restaurant was awful.

5. Judy likes movies. The movies are sad.

6. Buy this smart phone. The smart phone is cool.

7. Jeremy bought a flat-screen TV. The flat-screen TV was expensive.

8. Bill and Mark have jobs. The jobs are important.

EXERCISE 5: Adjective Modifiers with Plural Nouns

Rewrite the sentences. Make the nouns plural. Make all other necessary changes.

1. The personal ad is funny. *The personal ads are funny.*

2. He is an interesting man. _____

3. The black dog is friendly. _____

4. The expensive car is over there. _____

5. The artistic student is a young Italian. _____

6. The boring book has a red cover. _____

7. The middle-aged actor is from China. _____

EXERCISE 6: Adjective Modifiers

Write sentences. Use the words from columns A, D, and E only one time each.

A	B	C	D	E
~~Brad Pitt~~			~~American~~	~~actor~~
Beijing and Mexico City			beautiful	artist
Ferraris and BMWs	is		big	book
Prince Harry and Prince William	are	(a)	British	cars
Quebec	was	(an)	expensive	cities
Sushi	were		Japanese	food
The Beatles			old	men
The Bible			poor	place
Van Gogh			young	singers

1. *Brad Pitt is an American actor.* _____

2. _____

3. _____

4. _____

5. _____

6. _____

7. _____

8. _____

9. _____

EXERCISE 7: Editing

Correct the conversation. There are seven mistakes. The first mistake is already corrected. Find and correct six more.

A: Where were you last night?

B: I had a date.

A: Really?

B: Yeah. I met ^a beautiful woman through a personal ad.

(continued on next page)

A: Oh, yeah? Tell me about her. Is she an active like you?

B: Yeah. She plays three differents sports.

A: What else?

B: Well, she's a person very funny, and she listens to olds songs like I do.

A: Does she work?

B: Yeah. She has a interesting job with a music company.

A: She sounds like she's the woman perfect for you.

B: She is.

EXERCISE 8: Personal Writing

Write four sentences that describe a friend or family member.

> EXAMPLE: *My husband is a sushi chef. He is a fun-loving man. He loves spy movies. He's a very smart guy.*

1. _____

2. _____

3. _____

4. _____

UNIT 29 Comparative Adjectives

EXERCISE 1: Text Completion

Complete the conversation. Use the words from the box. Don't look at your Student Book.

better	cheaper	funny	more	snack	them
beverages	entertainment	~~invitations~~	older	than	worse

KEN: So when's the party?

LAURA: Saturday night about 8:00.

MARTY: How many people are coming? Did you send

_____*invitations*_____?
        1.

LAURA: Yeah. I've got 15 on the list.

MARTY: What about music? I can bring my rap and

heavy metal CDs.

KEN: Get real! We want to dance, right? Rap

is bad for dancing, and heavy metal is

_____. Any other kind of pop
    2.

music is _____ for dancing.
        3.

MI YOUNG: Let's have hip-hop then.

LAURA: OK. My _____ brother has a lot
        4.

of hip-hop CDs. Now, what about food and

snacks?

KEN: How about steak? We can barbecue some steak. And chips are fine for a

_____.
    5.

MI YOUNG: Let's get pizza. It's easier and quicker _____ steak. And it's
           6.

_____.
  7.

(continued on next page)

157

LAURA: OK. What about desserts and _____8._____?

MI YOUNG: We've got ice cream and we've got soda and juice.

KEN: What about _____9._____? Besides dancing, I mean.

MARTY: How about watching some DVDs?

LAURA: Well . . . I'm tired of _____10._____. Games are _____11._____ interesting than DVDs, at a party.

KEN: Hey, I know a really _____12._____ new game. It's called, "Who's faster? Who's smarter? Who's funnier?" We can play that.

EXERCISE 2: Vocabulary

What do you think? Complete the sentences with the words in parentheses.

1. (soda / water) _____Soda_____ is worse for you than _____water_____.

2. (entertainment / food) At a party, _____ is more important than _____.

3. (hip-hop / pop music) _____ is better than _____.

4. (desserts / snacks) _____ are more expensive than _____.

5. (beverages / pizza) _____ are cheaper than _____.

6. (books / games) _____ are more boring than _____.

EXERCISE 3: Adjectives with One, Two, or more than Two Syllables

Write each word from the box in the correct column on the next page.

active	busy	difficult	friendly	honest	old
artistic	cold	exciting	funny	important	short
boring	dark	expensive	healthy	interesting	warm

ONE SYLLABLE	TWO SYLLABLES, ENDING IN -Y	TWO SYLLABLES, NOT ENDING IN -Y	MORE THAN TWO SYLLABLES
		active	

EXERCISE 4: Comparative Adjectives: Regular and Irregular

Write the comparative forms of the adjectives.

1. old _____older_____   **6.** good _____

2. funny _____   **7.** important _____

3. quick _____   **8.** expensive _____

4. bad _____   **9.** heavy _____

5. famous _____   **10.** cheap _____

EXERCISE 5: Comparative Adjectives

Complete the sentences. Use the comparative forms of the adjectives.

1. This book is interesting, but the other book is ____more interesting____.

2. I'm busy on Mondays, but I'm _____ on Tuesdays.

3. English is difficult, but Chinese is _____.

4. Julia is short, but her sister is _____.

5. The movie is funny, but the book is _____.

6. Pop music is good, but hip-hop is _____.

7. This game is boring, but that game is _____.

8. My grandfather is active, but my grandmother is _____.

9. The traffic today is bad, but the traffic yesterday was _____.

10. It's cold today, but it was _____ yesterday.

EXERCISE 6: Comparative Adjectives + *Than*

Use comparative forms of the words from the box to make comparisons. Use each word only once.

bad	cheap	friendly	old	small
~~big~~	crowded	important	quick	warm

1. China is _____ *bigger than* _____ Japan.

2. Good health is _____ money.

3. An airplane moves quickly. An airplane is _____ a car.

4. An adult is _____ a child.

5. The weather in Greece is _____ the weather in Canada.

6. A big city is _____ a small town.

7. A golf ball is _____ a soccer ball.

8. The traffic in big cities is _____ the traffic in small cities.

9. I can buy a bicycle, but I can't buy a car. A bicycle is _____ a car.

10. I like dogs more than cats. Dogs are _____ cats.

EXERCISE 7: Questions with *Which*

*Write questions about comparisons. Use **which** and the words in parentheses. Then write answers.*

1. (expensive / computers or cell phones)

   Which are more expensive, computers or cell phones?   _Computers._

2. (easy / swimming or water skiing)

   _____   _____

3. (fast / planes or trains)

   _____   _____

4. (warm / India or Russia)

   _____   _____

160   UNIT 29

5. (popular around the world / soccer or baseball)

_____   _____

6. (healthy / candy or fruit)

_____   _____

EXERCISE 8: Editing

Correct the conversation. There are seven mistakes. The first mistake is already corrected. Find and correct six more.

A: So how's your new apartment? Is it ~~more good~~ _better_ than your old one?

B: Yes, it is. It's larger and more cheap.

A: And where is it? Is the location good?

B: Oh, yeah. It's near the train station, so it's more easy for me to get to work. And I like the neighborhood too. It has a lot of trees and is beautifuler. It's also more cleaner.

A: How many bedrooms are there in your apartment?

B: Well, there are three bedrooms. One bedroom is smaller from the other two. It's noisyer too. But the rest of the apartment is perfect. Why don't you come and see it this weekend?

A: That sounds like a good idea.

EXERCISE 9: Personal Writing

Write sentences that compare two people in your family. Use comparative adjectives.

EXAMPLE: My father is older than my mother.

1. _____

2. _____

3. _____

4. _____

EXERCISE 1: Text Completion

Complete the conversations. Use the words from the box. Don't look at your Student Book.

afternoon	barbecue	in	~~me~~	on	two-story
at	free	looking	1:00	Saturday	volleyball

TIM: Tim Olson.

FELIX: Hello, Tim! This is Felix Maxa. Do you remember

_____*me*_____? We met _____
　　　　　　　1.　　　　　　　　　　　　　　　2.

June on the train to Seattle.

TIM: Felix! Of course! It's great to hear from you. How

are you doing?

FELIX: Wonderful. Say, I called to invite you and your wife

to our house for a _____.
　　　　　　　　　　　　　　3.

TIM: That sounds like fun. We'd really like that. When is it?

FELIX: On _____, the 20th, in the _____.
　　　　　　　　4.　　　　　　　　　　　　　　　　5.

TIM: I think we're _____. But I need to check with Jessica. Can I call you back?
　　　　　　　　　　　6.

FELIX: Sure.

[Later—phone rings]

FELIX: Hello?

TIM: Hi, Felix. This is Tim. We're free _____ the 20th. We can come to the
　　　　　　　　　　　　　　　　　　　　7.

barbecue.

FELIX: Great!

TIM: What's the address?

FELIX: We're at 819 40th Avenue. From 45th, turn left on Stone Way and then right on

40th. It's the third house on the right, a light blue _____.
　　　　　　　　　　　　　　　　　　　　　　　　　8.

TIM: OK. What time?

FELIX: We're going to eat about 2:00. Why don't you come _____ 1:00?
9.
We can talk for a while.

TIM: Great. Can we bring anything?

FELIX: Maybe your sneakers. We're going to play _____.
10.

TIM: OK. Thanks a lot. I'm _____ forward to it. See you on Saturday at
11.
_____. Bye.
12.

FELIX: Good-bye.

EXERCISE 2: Vocabulary

Complete the sentences with the phrases from the box.

a two-story house	are looking forward to	go to a play	~~Of course~~
are free	go shopping	have a barbecue	play volleyball

1. _____Of course_____ Tim remembers Felix. They talked a lot on the train to
Seattle.

2. Tim and Jessica _____ on the 20th in the afternoon. They can
go to Felix's house.

3. They _____ seeing Felix.

4. Felix and his family often _____ on weekends. They usually
cook steak.

5. Jessica can _____ on Saturday morning. She needs some new
clothes.

6. Tim likes to _____ in the evening with his friends. It's good
exercise.

7. On Sunday, Tim and Jessica want to _____. They love the
theater.

8. Felix and his family live in _____, but Tim and Jessica live in
an apartment.

EXERCISE 3: Prepositions of Time

Write **in, on,** *or* **at** *before each word or phrase.*

1. _on_ weeknights
2. ____ 2:15
3. ____ Thursdays
4. ____ October 24, 2008
5. ____ May
6. ____ the evening
7. ____ a few minutes
8. ____ June 1st

9. ____ 1990
10. ____ the morning
11. ____ lunchtime
12. ____ 4:00
13. ____ November 3rd
14. ____ about 3:00
15. ____ the 15th
16. ____ night

EXERCISE 4: Prepositions of Time

Complete the conversation. Use **in, on,** *or* **at.**

LIZA: I'd like information about flights to Vancouver.

AGENT: When would you like to go?

LIZA: I'm not sure. I'd like to go _____*in*_____ September—either
1.

_____ September 19th or _____ September 20th.
2.   3.

AGENT: Well, September 19th is _____ a Sunday, so the ticket is cheaper.
4.

Tickets _____ weekdays are more expensive than tickets
5.

_____ the weekends.
6.

LIZA: Really? Well, when are there flights _____ Sunday, September 19th?
7.

AGENT: There's one _____ 7:00 _____ the morning, another
8.   9.

_____ noon, one flight _____ the afternoon
10.   11.

_____ 3:30, and another one _____ 9:00
12.   13.

_____ night.
14.

Look at Josh's calendar. Complete the sentences.

NOVEMBER						
Sunday	Monday	Tuesday	Wednesday	Thursday	Friday	Saturday
		1 library 7:00 P.M. gym	**2** 8:00 English class 2:00 math class	**3** a play with Diego	**4** library 7:00 P.M. gym	**5** volleyball
6 volleyball	**7** 8:00 English class	**8** library 7:00 P.M. gym	**9** 8:00 English class 2:00 math class 7:00 P.M. gym	**10** 7:00 P.M. gym	**11** library 7:00 P.M. gym	**12** volleyball
13 volleyball	**14** 8:00 English class 7:00 P.M. gym	**15** library	**16** 8:00 English class 2:00 math class	**17** Mom's birthday— She turns 45!	**18** library dentist appointment	**19** volleyball
20 volleyball	**21** 8:00 English class	**22** library	**23** 8:00 English class 2:00 math class	**24** 7:00 P.M. gym	**25** library barbecue	**26** volleyball
27 volleyball	**28** 8:00 English class	**29** library 7:00 P.M. gym	**30** 8:00 English class 2:00 math class			

1. Josh goes to math class ____*at*____ 2:00 _____*in the afternoon*_____ on Wednesdays.

2. Josh goes to the library _____.

3. Josh plays volleyball _____.

4. Josh is going to a play _____.

5. Josh has a barbecue _____.

6. Josh's mother's birthday is _____ Thursday, _____.

7. Josh is studying English and math _____ November.

8. Josh's English class is _____ 8:00 _____ the morning _____ Mondays and Wednesdays.

9. Josh often goes to the gym _____.

10. Josh has a dentist appointment _____.

Answer the questions. Write true long answers. Use **in, on,** *or* **at.**

1. What time do you get up? _I get up at 7:30 in the morning._
2. What time do you go to bed? _____
3. What year were you born? _____
4. What month were you born? _____
5. When is your birthday? _____
6. When did your parents get married? _____
7. What time does English class start and end? _____
8. What days do you have English class? _____
9. What time in the evening are you usually free? _____
10. When do you spend time with your family? _____

EXERCISE 7: Editing

Correct the conversations. There are eight mistakes. The first mistake is already corrected. Find and correct seven more.

1. **A:** When does class start?

   B: ~~On~~ At 2:00.

2. **A:** Is your birthday on May?

   B: Yes, it is. It's on May 20th.

3. **A:** Do you ever work at the night?

   B: Sometimes. But I usually work in morning.

4. **A:** When is your barbecue?

   B: It's in 5:00 at the evening.

5. **A:** What do you do in weekends?

   B: In Saturdays I go shopping.

EXERCISE 8: Personal Writing

Write an email invitation for a party. Say what type of party it is, when it is, and where it is. Use **in, on,** *and* **at** *in your invitation.*

EXAMPLE: *Come to my birthday party on Saturday, April 21st. It's at Skate Heaven on Park Street and 3rd Avenue. The party starts at eleven o'clock in the morning. I hope you can come.*

_____

_____

_____

_____

UNIT 31

Future with *Be going to*: Statements

EXERCISE 1: Text Completion

Complete the conversation. Use the words from the box. Don't look at your Student Book.

~~be~~	game	it's	not	soccer	start
football	going	little	player	sport	to

LAURA: Ken, hurry up! We're going to _____be_____ late!
_____ 1.

KEN: What's the hurry? It's just a silly little soccer _____!
_____ 2.

LAURA: It's not silly, and it's not _____.
_____ 3.
Sam's on the team! It's a big game. I think they're
_____ to win.
_____ 4.

KEN: I know. That's what you told me. Is your brother a good _____?
_____ 5.

LAURA: He's really good.

KEN: Do I need an umbrella?

LAURA: No. It's _____ going to rain . . . Come on.
_____ 6.

[Later]

LAURA: Can you drive any faster?

KEN: I'm already doing the speed limit. But how come you like _____ so much?
_____ 7.

LAURA: It's a great game. A lot of people can play it. You don't have to be a giant.

KEN: But is it a real sport? Take baseball or basketball or _____. Those are sports.
8.

LAURA: Soccer is the most popular _____ in the world.
9.

KEN: Well, _____ not the most popular sport in *my* world.
10.

LAURA: Oh, no! A traffic jam! The game's going to _____ soon.
11.

KEN: Laura, chill out! We're going _____ make it on time.
12.

EXERCISE 2: Vocabulary

Write the words in the correct columns.

~~baseball~~	gymnastics	skiing
basketball	hockey	soccer
football	running	swimming

This is a team sport.	This is not usually a team sport.
baseball	

Look at the pictures. Circle the correct statements.

1. a. He's falling.
   (b.) He's going to fall.

2. a. It's raining.
   b. It's going to rain.

3. a. He's sleeping.
   b. He's going to sleep.

4. a. She's playing hockey.
   b. She's going to play hockey.

5. a. He's watching TV.
   b. He's going to watch TV.

6. a. She's buying something.
   b. She's going to buy something.

EXERCISE 4: Future with *Be going to*: Affirmative Statements

*Look at the pictures. What are the people going to do? Complete the sentences about the future. Use **going to** and the words from the box.*

buy some food	have a party	see a movie	~~swim~~
exercise	have lunch	sleep	ski

1. They're _____*going to swim*_____.

2. They're _____.

3. He's _____.

4. They're _____.

5. He's _____.

6. She's _____.

(continued on next page)

7. He's _____.

8. They're _____.

Make negative sentences. Use **be going to** *and the verbs in parentheses.*

1. Mr. Olson __isn't going to see__ OR __'s not going to see__ the dentist this week. He saw the
             (see)
dentist last week.

2. Jessica _____ too much money on a gift. She spent too much
            (spend)
last time.

3. My friends and I _____ a movie tonight. We saw a movie last
             (watch)
night.

4. Mr. Lane _____ basketball today. He's going to play next week.
           (play)

5. My parents and I _____ my grandparents this weekend. We're
             (visit)
going to visit them next weekend.

6. Jeremy _____ a test next week. He's taking a test this week.
            (take)

Write sentences about your activities next weekend. Use **be going to** *and the words in parentheses.*

1. (clean my home) __I'm going to clean my home next weekend.__ OR __I'm not going to clean my__
   __home next weekend.__

2. (eat out) _____

3. (go out with friends) _____

4. (go shopping) _____

5. (go to a play) _____

6. (play baseball) _____

7. (have a barbecue) _____

8. (visit relatives) _____

9. (wake up early) _____

10. (work) _____

EXERCISE 7: Editing

Correct the paragraph. There are six mistakes. The first mistake is already corrected.
Find and correct five more.

                                                   It's

    I can't believe the course is almost over. ~~It~~ going to end in one week. Most of my

classmates are going return home, but some are no going to leave. Rana going to start

a new job. Misha is going to taking another course. Masao and Laura is going to get

married, and I'm going to go to their wedding.

EXERCISE 8: Personal Writing

Write four sentences about your plans for next weekend.

    EXAMPLE: *On Sunday morning I'm going to sleep late. In the afternoon, I'm going to play baseball*
with some friends. After the game, we're going to go to a pizza place. In the evening,
I'm probably going to watch TV.

1. _____

2. _____

3. _____

4. _____

EXERCISE 1: Text Completion

Complete the conversation. Use the words from the box. Don't look at your Student Book.

Are	be	~~How~~	isn't	news	to travel
are you	going	I'm	It's	producer	Who's

Tim: _____**How**_____ was your day?
1.

Jessica: Actually, I had an interesting call.

Tim: Oh?

Jessica: You know Dan Evans, the TV

_____?
2.

Tim: Sure I do.

Jessica: Well, he has an idea for a _____
3.

program.

Tim: Really?

Jessica: Uh-huh. _____ going to be on national TV, and he wants me to
4.

be in it.

Jeremy: Awesome! _____ you going to have a big part?
5.

Jessica: As a matter of fact, yes. I'm going to _____ the star.
6.

Jeremy: That's so cool. When _____ going to begin?
7.

Jessica: Not for a while.

Tim: Are you going _____ a lot?
8.

Jessica: I think so.

Annie: Don't take it, Mom. I don't want you to travel. I want you to stay home.

Ben: Yeah. You always help me with homework. _____ going to help
9.

me with my homework? How are you _____ to take me to soccer
10.

practice?

174

Tim: Hey, guys. _____ still going to be here.
11.

Jessica: Anyway, kids, this is all very new. The show _____ going to air for a
12.
long time.

EXERCISE 2: Vocabulary

Circle the correct answer.

1. George Henry is a movie producer. Are you going to see him in a movie?
   a. yes   **(b.)** no

2. Martha Sim is a TV producer. Is she going to spend a lot of money?
   a. yes   **b.** no

3. *Animal World* is going to be on national TV tonight. Who is going to watch it?
   a. only people in your city   **b.** people in different cities in your country

4. An actor has a big part in a movie. How many times are you going to see him in the movie?
   a. many times   **b.** not many times

5. Your friend says, "I'm nervous about the test tomorrow." What are you going to say?
   a. That's awesome.   **b.** Don't worry.

6. Your friend says, "I'm going to go on vacation next week." What are you going to say?
   a. That's too bad.   **b.** That's awesome.

7. You are going to watch a program. Where are you going to see it?
   a. at a movie theater   **b.** on TV

8. You are going to watch the news. What are you going to find out?
   a. information about TV shows   **b.** information about what is happening

EXERCISE 3: Future with *Be going to: Yes / No* Questions

Match the questions and answers.

_e_ **1.** Is Jeremy going to be late for school?

_____ **2.** Are you going to watch the news?

_____ **3.** Are we going to go out to eat?

_____ **4.** Are they going to take a trip?

_____ **5.** Is the baby going to come with us?

_____ **6.** Is she going to drive you?

_____ **7.** Am I going to like the program?

_____ **8.** Is Annie going to play in the game?

a. Yes, they're going to leave tomorrow.

b. Yes, it's always good.

c. No, I'm going to take the bus.

d. Yes, she's going to play today.

e. No, he's going to be on time.

f. No, I'm tired.

g. Yes, she is.

h. No, Dad's going to cook.

EXERCISE 4: Future with *Be going to: Yes / No* Questions and Short Answers

*Write **yes / no** questions with **be going to**. Then write short answers. Use the information in parentheses.*

1. A: _Is it going to be cold tonight?_ _____

   B: _Yes, it is._ _____ (It's going to be cold tonight.)

2. A: _____

   B: _____ (Laura Olson is going to get a big part in the play.)

3. A: _____

   B: _____ (You and your classmates aren't going to study

   tomorrow.)

4. A: _____

   B: _____ (Josh's parents are going to move next year.)

5. A: _____

   B: _____ (Tim is going to get a haircut.)

6. A: _____

   B: _____ (You're not going to stay in bed today.)

EXERCISE 5: Future with *Be going to: Wh-* Questions

Look at the picture. Write questions. Use the words in parentheses and **be going to.**
Then write the letter of the correct answer next to each question.

a. The owner of the car.	**e.** The man in the black shirt.
b. At 5:00.	**f.** ~~Write a parking ticket.~~
c. On a ski vacation.	**g.** Angry.
d. Because they're going to see a movie.	**h.** The woman's wallet.

_f_ **1.** (What / the police officer / do) _____ What is the police officer going to do? _____

____ **2.** (Who / get / a ticket _____

____ **3.** (Who / take / something from the old woman) _____

____ **4.** (What / the man in the black shirt / take) _____

____ **5.** (How / the old woman / feel) _____

____ **6.** (Where / the owner of the car / go) _____

____ **7.** (Why / the people / go into the movie theater) _____

____ **8.** (When / the movie / start) _____

EXERCISE 6: Future with *Be going to: Wh-* Questions

Complete the conversations. Write questions with **be going to.** *Use* **how, what, when, where,** *or* **who** *and the words in parentheses.*

1. **A:** Jessica is going to be on national TV.

   B: (work for) _Who is she going to work for?_ _____

   A: Dan Evans, the TV producer.

2. **A:** Dan has an idea for a news program.

   B: (start) _____

   A: Not for a long time.

3. **A:** I'm going to go to the supermarket.

   B: (buy) _____

   A: Some soda, some ice cream, and some other things for the party.

4. **A:** We're going to go to the city next weekend.

   B: (get there) _____

   A: One of my friends is going to drive us.

5. **A:** Melissa is going to go on vacation soon.

   B: (go) _____

   A: To Thailand.

6. **A:** The house is very messy.

   B: (clean it) _____

   A: My dad and I.

EXERCISE 7: Future with *Be going to: Wh-* Questions

Answer the questions. Write true answers.

1. How long is your next class going to be? _____

2. Who is going to meet you later? _____

3. What time are you going to go to bed tonight? _____

4. Where are you going to go tomorrow? _____

5. How are you going to get there? _____

6. Who are you going to spend time with next weekend? _____

7. When is your next test going to be? _____

EXERCISE 8: Editing

Correct the conversation. There are nine mistakes. The first mistake is already corrected. Find and correct eight more.

A: Did you hear the news? Amanda's pregnant.

B: That's awesome. When ~~she is~~ *is she* going to have the baby?

A: At the end of January. She's going to stopping work in the middle of December.

B: Are we going have a party for her?

A: Yes. We going to have it in early December.

B: Wow, Amanda and her husband are to have a baby!

A: It going to be very exciting for them.

B: What is she and Josh going to name the baby?

A: I have no idea.

B: Where they going to live? They are going to move?

A: I think so. Their apartment is very small.

EXERCISE 9: Personal Writing

Which famous person do you want to meet? Think of four questions to ask that person about the future. Write the questions with **be going to.**

EXAMPLE: *When are you going to make your next movie? Who is going to be in it? Are you going to marry your boyfriend? Where are you going to live?*

1. _____

2. _____

3. _____

4. _____

WORKBOOK ANSWER KEY

In this answer key, where the full form is given, the contraction is also acceptable. Where the contracted form is given, the full form is also acceptable, unless the exercise is about contractions.

UNIT 1 (pages 1–5)

EXERCISE 1

2. This	**6.** This is	**10.** family
3. It's	**7.** These are	**11.** These
4. are	**8.** is	**12.** husband
5. They're	**9.** We're	

EXERCISE 2

3. son / brother
4. daughter / sister / wife / mother
5. husband / father
6. son / brother
7. daughter / sister
8. son / brother

EXERCISE 3

2. It	**5.** She	**8.** It
3. I	**6.** He	**9.** We
4. It	**7.** They	**10.** They

EXERCISE 4

2. f	**4.** g	**6.** c	**8.** d
3. a	**5.** b	**7.** h	

EXERCISE 5

2. This is your pencil.
3. Is this your ticket?
4. These are your keys.
5. This is my house.
6. Is this your apartment?
7. Are these your friends?
8. These are your seats.

EXERCISE 6

2. a	**4.** b	**6.** a
3. b	**5.** a	

EXERCISE 7

2. **A:** ~~These are~~ *Are these* your keys?
   B: Yes. Thank you.
3. **A:** This is my car.
   B: ~~She~~ *It* is big.

4. **A:** ~~This~~ *These* are my books.
   B: Oh. Sorry.
5. **A:** These are my ~~pet~~ *pets*.
   B: They're nice.
6. **A:** Is this your sister?
   B: Yes, her name is Mary. ~~He~~ *She* is a teacher.

EXERCISE 8

Answers will vary.

UNIT 2 (pages 6–10)

EXERCISE 1

2. a	**6.** Is	**10.** They're
3. toaster	**7.** are	**11.** teacher
4. an	**8.** these	**12.** I'm
5. this	**9.** What	

EXERCISE 2

2. an egg	**5.** a muffin	**8.** an oven
3. a knife	**6.** an apple	**9.** a stove
4. a glass	**7.** a refrigerator	

EXERCISE 3

A.
2. This apple is from Canada.
3. This child is from Haiti.
4. The muffin is on the counter.
5. The glass is in the kitchen.
B.
2. These people are from Mexico.
3. These girls are from Japan.
4. These knives are from Austria.
5. These teachers are from China.

EXERCISE 4

2. glass	**6.** knife
3. brother	**7.** classes
4. children	**8.** dishes
5. friends	

181

EXERCISE 5

2. **B:** No. They're from (Hawaii).
3. **A:** This is an oven.
   B: No, it isn't. It's a stove.
4. **A:** Is this an apple?
   B: Yes. It's an apple.
5. **A:** Is (Judy) from (Canada)?
   B: No. She's from (England)
6. **A:** Is (Mr. Lopez) a student?
   B: No. He's a teacher.

EXERCISE 6

2. **A:** Is Jessica ~~from a China~~? *from China*
   B: Yes, she's ^*a* student in my class.
3. **A:** These ~~are a forks~~. *are forks*
   B: No, they aren't. They're spoons. This is ^*a* fork.
4. **A:** This ~~refrigerators~~ is big. *refrigerator*
   B: Yes, it is.
5. **A:** ~~These~~ is my kitchen. *This*
   B: It's big!
6. **A:** What's this?
   B: It's ~~a~~ orange. *an*

EXERCISE 7

Answers will vary.

UNIT 3 (pages 11–16)

EXERCISE 1

2. is
3. They're
4. not
5. Australia
6. you
7. from
8. am
9. clean
10. delicious
11. It's
12. I

EXERCISE 2

2. isn't / 's
3. isn't / 's
4. 'm / 'm not
5. isn't / 's
6. 're not / 're

EXERCISE 3

√ - 3, 5, 7, 8

EXERCISE 4

3. isn't
4. isn't
5. is
6. is
7. is
8. is

EXERCISE 5

2. is
3. is
4. is
5. are
6. are
7. are
8. is
9. am
10. is

EXERCISE 6

2. It is terrible there.
3. She is not popular.
4. We are not here on business.
5. You are friendly.
6. They are not from Seattle.

EXERCISE 7

2. We're from Tokyo.
3. They're not here.
   OR They aren't here.
4. I'm not the teacher.
5. He's my cousin.
6. You're from here.

EXERCISE 8

2. **A:** ~~The~~ food good? *Is the*
   B: ~~Is~~ terrible. *It's*
3. **A:** This ^ my cousin. *is*
   B: ~~Are~~ she a student? *Is*
4. **A:** ~~Be~~ you from Mexico? *Are*
   B: No, we're ~~are~~ from Peru.
5. **A:** ~~Your~~ cousins Amy and Mary ~~are~~ here on vacation? *Are your*
   B: No, ~~they~~ here on business. *they're*

EXERCISE 9

Answers will vary.

UNIT 4 (pages 17–21)

EXERCISE 1

2. How about
3. isn't
4. her
5. those
6. stadiums
7. Are
8. your
9. building
10. its
11. It's
12. a great idea

EXERCISE 2

2. g
3. d
4. b
5. a
6. h
7. e
8. f

EXERCISE 3

1. that / That
2. those / Those
3. this / that
4. This / these / These
5. this / this

EXERCISE 4

2. my
3. Their
4. my OR our
5. His
6. My OR Our
7. her
8. Her

EXERCISE 5

2. b
3. a
4. a
5. b
6. a

EXERCISE 6

2. **A:** Are ~~that~~ *those* your children?
   B: No, ~~their~~ *they're* my brother's son and daughter.
3. **A:** ~~Is~~ *Are* those your glasses?
   B: No, ~~these~~ *they're* my sunglasses.
4. **A:** ~~That~~ *Those* people are teachers.
   B: ~~His~~ *Their* names are Steve Beck and Annie Macintosh.
5. **A:** ~~That is~~ *Is that* your cousin?
   B: Yes, ~~she~~ *her* name is Jessica.

EXERCISE 7

Answers will vary.

UNIT 5 (pages 22–27)

EXERCISE 1

2. Yes
3. it
4. Who's
5. Is
6. he is
7. does
8. He's
9. Her
10. she
11. she's
12. What

EXERCISE 2

2. b
3. a
4. b
5. a
6. a

EXERCISE 3

Conversation 1

A: Who's that woman?
B: That's Amy. She's my teacher.
A: Is she a good teacher?
B: Yes. And she's friendly too.
A: What's her last name?
B: Diaz.

Conversation 2

A: Is that your wife?
B: Yes. Her name's Ellen.
A: What does she do?
B: She's a writer.
A: What does she write?
B: Travel books.

EXERCISE 4

2. Is she your sister?
3. Who is that woman?
4. Is your father a dentist?
5. What is their last name?
6. What does your friend do?

EXERCISE 5

2. Yes, I am. OR No, I'm not.
3. Yes, I am. OR No, I'm not.
4. Yes, she/he is. OR No, she/he isn't. OR No, she's/ he's not.
5. Yes, she/he is. OR No, she/he isn't. OR No, she's/ he's not.
6. Yes, it is. OR No, it isn't. OR No, it's not.
7. Yes, they are. OR No, they aren't. OR No, they're not.
8. Yes, we are. OR No, we aren't. OR No, we're not.

EXERCISE 6

2. Who, Ben.
3. Who, My grandchildren.
4. What, A camera.

EXERCISE 7

2. What, His name is Peter.
3. What, It's Canberra.
4. Who, It's Lynn Martin.

EXERCISE 8

2. **A:** ~~You~~ *Are you* and Joe married?
   B: Yes, ~~we're~~ *we are*.
3. **A:** Who ~~be~~ *is* that boy?
   B: ~~That~~ *That's* my son.
4. **A:** ~~Who~~ *What* is the capital of the United States?
   B: ~~Is~~ *It's* Washington, D.C.
5. **A:** ~~That~~ *Is that* woman your mother?
   B: Yes, ~~she's~~ *she is*.
6. **A:** *Is* Bob a clerk ~~is~~?
   B: No, he isn't.

EXERCISE 9

Answers will vary.

EXERCISE 1

2. party	**6.** at	**10.** bus
3. Where's	**7.** from	**11.** corner
4. is	**8.** gym	**12.** Her
5. between	**9.** floor	

EXERCISE 2

2. hospital	**5.** library
3. restaurant	**6.** movie theater
4. museum	

EXERCISE 3

3. T	**5.** F	**7.** T
4. F	**6.** F	**8.** T

EXERCISE 4

2. post office	**6.** park
3. restaurant	**7.** supermarket
4. art museum	**8.** apartment building
5. movie theater	**9.** library

EXERCISE 5

2. Where are Mr. and Mrs. Lin from?
3. Where are the doctors from?
4. Where's Paul from? OR Where is Paul from?
5. Where are you from?

EXERCISE 6

Number	Word	Ordinal Number	Ordinal Word
1. 4	*four*	4th	fourth
2. 6	six	*6th*	*sixth*
3. 1	*one*	*1st*	first
4. 9	nine	*9th*	*ninth*
5. 8	*eight*	8th	*eighth*
6. 2	*two*	*2nd*	second
7. 3	three	*3rd*	*third*
8. 7	*seven*	7th	*seventh*
9. 10	*ten*	*10th*	tenth
10. 5	*five*	5th	*fifth*

EXERCISE 7

2. It's on the first floor.
3. It's on the third floor.
4. It's on the fourth floor.
5. It's on the sixth floor.
6. It's on the second floor.

EXERCISE 8

What's your phone number, and ~~what's~~ *where's* your

apartment? Is it on Main Street? And what floor is

your apartment ~~in~~ *on*?

My phone number *is* 555–0900. My apartment

isn't ~~at~~ Main Street. It's ~~on~~ *at* 212 Park Avenue.

Take the number 12 bus. My apartment

building is next *to* the post office, and my

apartment is on the ~~nine~~ *ninth* floor.

EXERCISE 9

Answers will vary.

EXERCISE 1

2. last	**6.** movies	**10.** was
3. weren't	**7.** Were	**11.** funny
4. you	**8.** I wasn't	**12.** it
5. wasn't	**9.** Were you	

EXERCISE 2

2. a	**4.** c	**6.** f
3. g	**5.** b	**7.** d

EXERCISE 3

Answers will vary.

EXERCISE 4

3. [I'm happy today, but] I wasn't happy yesterday.
4. [It's cold today, but] it wasn't cold yesterday.
5. [The children are not at a soccer game today, but] they were at a soccer game yesterday.
6. [We aren't tired today, but] we were tired yesterday.
7. [The streets aren't dirty today, but] they were dirty yesterday.
8. [You're at the library today, but] you weren't at the library yesterday.

9. [I'm not home today, but] I was home yesterday.
10. [The boys are at the movies today, but] they weren't at the movies yesterday.

EXERCISE 5

2. wasn't   5. was   8. wasn't
3. was   6. was   9. were
4. were   7. weren't

EXERCISE 6

Answers for B may vary.

2. **A:** Was Jeremy at a soccer game yesterday?
   B: Yes, he was. It was exciting
3. **A:** Were Tim and Jessica at a play yesterday?
   B: Yes, they were.
4. **A:** Was Judy at a party last night?
   B: No, she wasn't.
5. **A:** Was Mark at a soccer game yesterday?
   B: No, he wasn't.
6. **A:** Were Amy, Steve, and Jenny at a party last night?
   B: Yes, they were.

EXERCISE 7

1. **A:** ~~They were~~ *Were they* at home yesterday?
   B: Yes, they ~~was~~ *were*.
2. **A:** Hi. ~~How~~ *How's* it going?
   B: Great.
3. **A:** ~~Were~~ *Was* the movie funny yesterday?
   B: No, it ~~isn't~~ *wasn't*.
4. **A:** Where were you ~~the~~ last night?
   B: ~~Was~~ *I was* at home.

EXERCISE 8

Answers will vary.

UNIT 8 (pages 41–45)

EXERCISE 1

2. you   6. weather   10. was
3. long   7. cool   11. Who
4. vacation 8. food   12. guide
5. were   9. tour

EXERCISE 2

2. It was cool and windy.
3. It was cold and sunny.
4. It was cold and cloudy.
5. It was warm and sunny.
6. It was hot and rainy.

EXERCISE 3

2. When   5. How
3. Where   6. How long
4. Who   7. Who

EXERCISE 4

Answers to the following questions will vary.

2. How long was your English class?
3. When were you at the supermarket?
4. How was the weather yesterday?
5. Where were you yesterday?
6. Who were you with last weekend?

EXERCISE 5

2. Fun. OR Great.
3. San Francisco. OR In San Francisco.
4. My brother and sister.
5. Five days. OR For five days.
6. Cool and rainy.

EXERCISE 6

2. **A:** ~~Who~~ *Where* were the students?
   B: They were in the classroom.
3. **A:** How long *was* class?
   B: Two hours.
4. **A:** How was the weather?
   B: ~~Was~~ *It was* sunny and warm.
5. **A:** When ~~was~~ *were* they here?
   B: Last Friday.
6. **A:** How ~~long~~ was the movie?
   B: It was very funny.

EXERCISE 7

Answers will vary.

UNIT 9 (pages 46–51)

EXERCISE 1

2. Don't   6. Turn   10. truck
3. Indian   7. right   11. Please
4. corner   8. Is   12. sign
5. go   9. park here

EXERCISE 2

2. a truck   6. park
3. a gas station 7. turn right
4. a bus stop   8. turn left
5. a restaurant

EXERCISE 3

2. b   **4.** b   **6.** a
3. a   **5.** a

EXERCISE 4

2. Listen to / Look at
3. Look at / Read
4. Answer / Ask / Listen to / Look at
5. Ask / Answer
6. Circle / Underline / Write

EXERCISE 5

Please *can go at the beginning or end of every sentence.*

3. Please don't open your books.
4. Drive me to school, please.
5. Please don't call me.
6. Don't close the windows, please.
7. Please give me a glass of water.
8. Help me with the bags, please.

EXERCISE 6

      Don't
2. A: ~~You no~~ go straight at the corner. Turn left.
    B: Got it.
3. A: Please ~~you~~ don't close the window. It's hot!
    B: Sure. No problem.
    Drive
4. A: ~~Drives~~ one block. Then turn ~~you~~ right.
    B: OK. Thanks.
    Please open
5. A: ~~Open please~~ the door.
    B: Sure.

EXERCISE 7

Answers will vary.

UNIT 10 (pages 52–56)

EXERCISE 1

2. is   **6.** have   **10.** watch
3. lives   **7.** like   **11.** surfs
4. teaches   **8.** likes   **12.** writes
5. looks   **9.** doesn't

EXERCISE 2

A. *Answers will vary*

B. *All of the sentences are false. There are 100 million or more native speakers of Arabic, English, Japanese, Mandarin Chinese, Portuguese, and Spanish. There are*

50 to 100 million native speakers of French, Italian, and Korean. There are 1 to 10 million native speakers of Swahili.

EXERCISE 3

2. b   **4.** b   **6.** b   **8.** a
3. a   **5.** c   **7.** c

EXERCISE 4

2. reports   **5.** drives
3. teaches   **6.** sings
4. likes   **7.** play

EXERCISE 5

2. doesn't have   **6.** doesn't want
3. don't speak   **7.** don't have
4. don't need   **8.** doesn't teach
5. don't like   **9.** doesn't rain

EXERCISE 6

2. I drink coffee. OR I don't drink coffee.
3. I read newspapers. OR I don't read newspapers.
4. I surf the Internet. OR I don't surf the Internet.
5. I watch TV. OR I don't watch TV.
6. I study a lot. OR I don't study a lot.

EXERCISE 7

2. looks   **12.** loves
3. doesn't look   **13.** doesn't love
4. have   **14.** speak
5. has   **15.** don't speak
6. work   **16.** speak
7. works   **17.** don't come
8. work   **18.** comes
9. doesn't work   **19.** comes
10. goes   **20.** speaks
11. fixes   **21.** doesn't speak

EXERCISE 8

              lives   *live*
My brother, Ken, ~~live~~ with my parents. They ~~lives~~
               has
in a big house. My father ~~have~~ a new car. He cleans his
         doesn't
car every day. Ken ~~not~~ have a new car. His car is old.
 doesn't   *loves*   *doesn't love*
It ~~don't~~ run, but he ~~love~~ it. My mother ~~no love~~ cars.
  loves   *works*
She ~~love~~ her garden. She ~~work~~ in it every Saturday
        don't
and Sunday. I ~~doesn't~~ see my family often, but we
talk on the weekends.

EXERCISE 9

Answers will vary.

EXERCISE 1

2.	flat screen	8.	Does
3.	want	9.	you
4.	Josh and I	10.	fix
5.	sale	11.	they do
6.	Do	12.	doesn't
7.	off		

EXERCISE 2

Answers will vary.

EXERCISE 3

2.	e	4.	a
3.	d	5.	b

EXERCISE 4

2.	Do	4.	Does	6.	Do
3.	Do	5.	Do		

EXERCISE 5

2.	f	4.	c	6.	e
3.	b	5.	a		

EXERCISE 6

3. No, she doesn't.
4. No, they don't.
5. No, she doesn't.
6. Yes, they do.
7. Yes, she does.
8. Yes, I do. OR No, I don't.
9. Yes, I do. OR No, I don't.

EXERCISE 7

2. Does she work on Sunday?
3. Does he speak Japanese?
4. Do they have a computer?
5. Does she know Kathy?
6. Do they need a new TV?
7. Does it fix cameras? OR Does the store fix cameras?
8. Do you speak Portuguese (at home)?

EXERCISE 8

2. **A:** Does the store have a service department?
   B: No, it doesn't.
3. **A:** Does Steve know a good electronics store?
   B: Yes, he does.
4. **A:** Do you like computer games?
   B: No, I don't.
5. **A:** Does Bob's Electronics have great deals?
   B: Yes, it does.

6. **A:** Does Nick spend a lot of time on the computer?
   B: Yes, he does.
7. **A:** Does it cost a lot to send text messages?
   B: No, it doesn't.
8. **A:** Does Judy want a gift?
   B: No, she doesn't.
9. **A:** Does Steve use his phone for a lot of things?
   B: Yes, he does.

EXERCISE 9

2.	Does he play	6.	I love
3.	Does your brother listen	7.	Jeremy doesn't like
4.	That's	8.	Do you have
5.	Do you like	9.	Jeremy loves

EXERCISE 10

2. **A:** Does your mother ~~has~~ *have* a smart phone?
   B: Yes, she ~~is~~ *does*.
3. **A:** ~~The~~ *Do the* three stores have great deals?
   B: One store ~~have~~ *has* great deals. The other two are expensive.
4. **A:** *Does* Focus on Grammar have a lot of grammar practice?
   B: Yes, it ~~has~~ *does*.
5. **A:** Do you and the other students like this book?
   B: No, we don't ~~like~~.

EXERCISE 11

Answers will vary.

EXERCISE 1

2.	do	6.	does	10.	what
3.	go	7.	time	11.	have
4.	stay up	8.	is	12.	start
5.	Why	9.	off		

EXERCISE 2

2.	g	5.	h	8.	f
3.	a	6.	e		
4.	b	7.	c		

EXERCISE 3

2. Who goes to school with you?
3. How do you get to school?
4. What do you study in school?
5. Why does your brother go to school early?
6. What time does your brother get home?
7. When do you play tennis?

EXERCISE 4

2. It's seven ten. OR It's ten after seven.
3. It's two (minutes) after three. OR It's three-oh-two.
4. It's four forty. OR It's twenty to five.
5. It's ten to nine. OR It's eight fifty.
6. It's five to eight. OR It's seven fifty-five.
7. It's eleven o'clock. OR It's eleven.
8. It's one thirty. OR It's half past one.
9. It's a quarter after two. OR It's two fifteen.
10. It's a quarter to seven. OR It's six forty-five.
11. It's twenty-five after ten. OR It's ten twenty-five.
12. It's twenty-five to four. OR It's three thirty-five.

EXERCISE 5

2. What does your mother do?
3. Why do you listen to jazz?
4. What time is dinner? OR What time do you eat dinner?
5. Why does he get up (so) early?
6. Where do your cousins live?
7. Who owns the restaurant?

EXERCISE 6

YUKO: What time *does* English class ~~starts~~ *start*?
OMAR: At 1:00.
YUKO: What time *does* class finish?
OMAR: At 2:30.
YUKO: What *does* ~~means~~ *dislike* *mean*?
OMAR: It means "not like."
YUKO: How *do* you say this word?
OMAR: I don't know.
YUKO: ~~Do~~ *Does* the teacher teach every day?
OMAR: No. She doesn't teach on Friday.
YUKO: What ~~have we~~ *do we have* for homework?
OMAR: Page 97.
YUKO: Why does Elena know all the answers?
OMAR: She ~~study~~ *studies* a lot.

EXERCISE 7

Answers will vary.

EXERCISE 1

2. She's	6. have	10. is
3. don't	7. are	11. has
4. look like	8. tall	12. pregnant
5. dark hair	9. thin	

EXERCISE 2

2. isn't / has
3. aren't / don't have
4. is / doesn't have
5. are / have
6. isn't / has
7. is / doesn't have
8. is / has

EXERCISE 3

2. have OR don't have
3. 'm OR 'm not
4. have OR don't have
5. have OR don't have
6. 'm OR 'm not
7. have OR don't have
8. 'm OR 'm not
9. 'm OR 'm not
10. have OR don't have

EXERCISE 4

2. is	6. is	10. have
3. is	7. has	11. have
4. isn't	8. doesn't have	12. are
5. is	9. is	

EXERCISE 5

3. What's the name of Bono's band?
4. Is Bono a violinist?
5. What's Bono's real name?
6. Where is he from?
7. Does he have any brothers or sisters?
8. Is he married?
9. Do they have children?
10. Where do they have a home?

EXERCISE 6

A: ~~What~~ *What's* your name?
B: Alice.
A: How old ~~have~~ *are* you?
B: I ~~have~~ *am* twenty-four.
A: ~~You~~ *Do you* have a big family?
B: Yes, I do. I have three sisters and four brothers.
A: Where do you live?
B: My home *is* near here. It's on Center Street.

A: Is <u>it</u> big?

it

B: No. ~~It~~ small. I live alone. My family lives in another city.

It's

Do you have

A: ~~Have you~~ a job?

B: No. I study at a university.

EXERCISE 7

Answers will vary.

UNIT 14 (pages 73–78)

EXERCISE 1

2. ever
3. Sometimes
4. always have
5. I sometimes
6. Rarely
7. have
8. I'm
9. usually go
10. always
11. often
12. times

EXERCISE 2

(crossword puzzle)

Across/Down answers:
- carrots
- vegetables
- fast food
- sweets
- ccc
- garden
- meat
- fish
- protein
- bottle
- etc.

EXERCISE 3

Answers will vary.

EXERCISE 4

2. Steve does not exercise often.
3. Bill rarely eats donuts.
4. It snows here sometimes. OR It sometimes snows here.
5. Mary is usually not busy. OR Mary is not busy, usually.
6. It is often hot in Cairo.

EXERCISE 5

2. I sometimes play soccer. OR I play soccer sometimes.
3. I am rarely late for class.
4. The food at that restaurant is never good.

5. Jennifer rarely sees a play.
6. Robert often goes to the movies. OR Robert goes to the movies often.

EXERCISE 6

2. Robert never cooks.
3. Nick usually goes to the gym. OR Usually, Nick goes to the gym. OR Nick goes to the gym, usually.
4. Mr. and Mrs. Lee sometimes go to a restaurant. OR Sometimes, Mr. and Mrs. Lee go to a restaurant. OR Mr. and Mrs. Lee go to a restaurant, sometimes.
5. Ruth always eats lunch.

EXERCISE 7

2. Do you ever go to the theater?
3. Do your children ever eat sweets?
4. How often do you listen to the radio?
5. Do you ever eat fast food?
6. How often does Tim cook fish?
7. Are you ever home on the weekend?

EXERCISE 8

Here is my schedule. I ~~usually am~~ busy on

am usually

Monday evenings. I ~~go often~~ to the gym, or I play

often go

basketball. (Do ~~ever you~~ play basketball?) On Fridays

you ever

~~always I~~ exercise too. I go dancing at the club! On

I always

Wednesdays and Thursdays I sometimes work late,

but I'm often free on Tuesdays. I finish work ~~usually~~

usually

at 5:30. Do you want to meet at <u>Vincenzo's</u> Italian Restaurant at 6:30 on Tuesday? The food there is

~~good always~~.

always good

EXERCISE 9

Answers will vary.

UNIT 15 (pages 79–83)

EXERCISE 1

2. were
3. living
4. He's
5. sitting
6. They're
7. not
8. is
9. texting
10. are
11. I'm
12. not working

EXERCISE 2

2. d **5.** b
3. f **6.** c
4. a

EXERCISE 3

2. closing **6.** fixing **10.** opening
3. doing **7.** looking **11.** running
4. stopping **8.** listening **12.** trying
5. enjoying **9.** moving

EXERCISE 4

2. are listening **6.** is helping
3. reading **7.** is working
4. is cooking **8.** is writing
5. is washing

EXERCISE 5

2. I'm wearing glasses right now. OR I'm not wearing glasses right now.
3. I'm texting right now. OR I'm not texting right now.
4. I'm sitting in my bedroom right now. OR I'm not sitting in my bedroom right now.
5. I'm eating right now. OR I'm not eating right now.
6. I'm sitting with my friend right now. OR I'm not sitting with my friend right now.
7. I'm drinking water right now. OR I'm not drinking water right now.
8. I'm looking at a computer right now. OR I'm not looking at a computer right now.

EXERCISE 6

It's
Hello from Seattle. ~~It~~ raining right now, but
we're having *sitting* *I'm*
~~we have~~ fun. Jenny and I are ~~sit~~ in a restaurant. ~~I~~
eating lunch. The food here in Seattle is good.
is not *is drinking* *talking*
Jenny ~~no is~~ eating. She ~~drink~~ coffee. We aren't ~~talk~~.
reading
Jenny's ~~read~~ the newspaper. I hope you're fine.

EXERCISE 7

Answers will vary.

UNIT 16 (pages 84–89)

EXERCISE 1

2. watching **8.** Is he
3. babysitting **9.** baking
4. How's **10.** studying
5. listening **11.** They're
6. are **12.** around
7. with

EXERCISE 2

2. g **5.** b
3. a **6.** c
4. e **7.** d

EXERCISE 3

2. Yes, it is. OR No, it's not. OR No, it isn't.
3. Yes, it is. OR No, it's not. OR No, it isn't.
4. Yes, I am. OR No, I'm not.
5. Yes, they are. OR No, they aren't. OR No, they're not.
6. Yes, I am. OR No, I'm not.
7. Yes, I am. OR No, I'm not.
8. Yes, I am. OR No, I'm not.

EXERCISE 4

2. A: Is he sleeping in his bedroom?
   B: No, he isn't. OR No, he's not.
3. A: Are the Smiths celebrating?
   B: Yes, they are.
4. A: Is Ben getting a haircut?
   B: No, he isn't. OR No, he's not.
5. A: Are the children cleaning the kitchen?
   B: No, they aren't. OR No, they're not.
6. A: Is Paula drinking coffee with milk?
   B: Yes, she is.

EXERCISE 5

3. Is Jessica cooking dinner? — Yes, she is.
4. Is the cat wearing a hat? — Yes, it is.
5. Are Ben and Annie playing cards? — Yes, they are.
6. Is Jeremy listening to music? — No, he isn't. OR No, he's not.
7. Is Tim writing a letter? — Yes, he is.
8. Is the cat sitting on the floor? — No, it isn't. OR No, it's not.
9. Is the cat reading? — Yes, it is.

EXERCISE 6

2. He's making **5.** Is he sleeping
3. Are your parents eating **6.** He's watching
4. My parents are having

EXERCISE 7

making
1. A: Are you ~~make~~ a mess?
    I'm
   B: No, ~~I~~ not.
    Is your sister
2. A: ~~Your sister~~ helping you with your homework?
    she is
   B: Yes, ~~she's~~.

3. A: Is Mr. Olson ~~work~~ *working*?

B: No, he isn't. He's ~~eat~~ *eating* lunch.

4. A: Is ~~sleeping Kelly~~ *Kelly sleeping*?

B: No, she's not. ~~She~~ *She's* watching a DVD with her friend.

5. A: ~~Is~~ *Are* Chris and Lee babysitting?

B: Yes, ~~they're~~ *they are*.

EXERCISE 8

Answers will vary.

UNIT 17 (pages 90–94)

EXERCISE 1

2. This	8. driving
3. are	9. doing
4. What	10. He's
5. planning	11. are you
6. traveling	12. Who
7. By	

EXERCISE 2

2. by bicycle	5. by train
3. by boat	6. by car
4. by bus	7. by subway

EXERCISE 3

2. Who	5. Why	7. What
3. What	6. How	8. Where
4. Where		

EXERCISE 4

2. Where is the family having a picnic? — On the grass by the pond.

3. What is Jeremy doing? — Listening to music.

4. Why are Jessica and Tim eating? — Because they're hungry.

5. How is everyone feeling? — Happy.

6. Where are Jessica and Tim sitting? — On a blanket.

7. Who is listening to music? — Jeremy.

8. What are Annie and Ben doing? — They're riding bikes.

EXERCISE 5

2. Who are you talking
3. What are you wearing
4. Who is traveling
5. Where is he teaching

EXERCISE 6

2. A: How *are* the people traveling?

B: ~~With~~ *By* boat.

3. A: Why ~~Nick is~~ *is Nick* wearing a suit?

B: Because ~~he~~ *he's* going to a job interview.

4. A: ~~What's~~ *How's* everything going?

B: Great. We are ~~have~~ *having* a lot of fun.

5. A: Where *are* Nick and Jerry ~~are~~ going?

B: To Denver.

6. A: Who's Jeremy ~~send~~ *sending* an email message to?

B: A friend from school.

EXERCISE 7

Answers will vary.

UNIT 18 (pages 95–99)

EXERCISE 1

2. parents'	8. those
3. That's	9. roommate's OR
4. that	brother's
5. brother's OR roommate's	10. This
6. fit	11. that's good
7. these	12. Kathy's

EXERCISE 2

3. earrings	6. slacks	9. belt
4. casual shoes	7. dress shoes	
5. tie	8. sports jacket	

EXERCISE 3

2. His parents' names are Bill and Mary.
3. Steve's apartment is in Seattle.
4. The students' tests are on the desk.
5. The teacher's book is in her bag.
6. Our daughters' husbands are very nice.
7. The children's room is on the second floor.
8. My roommate's cousins visit her every weekend.
9. Josh's tie goes well with his sports jacket.
10. Kathy's last name is White.

Workbook Answer Key **191**

EXERCISE 4

2. Who is wearing Mark's sports jacket?
3. That is not Sam's shirt.
4. The woman is not looking at the slacks.
5. *Not possible to change.*
6. Amanda is wearing new sunglasses.
7. It is Ben's tie.
8. Mark is nervous about his dinner with Kathy's parents.

EXERCISE 5

2. What are those? / These
3. *Answers will vary. Possible answers include:* What does this say? OR What's this?
4. What's that? / This

EXERCISE 6

2. **A:** The ~~women~~ *women's* rest room is over there.
   B: Thanks.
3. **A:** Who's ~~this~~ *that* over there?
   B: That's Ken.
4. **A:** Look at Mark over there. Does he usually wear ties?
   B: No. He's wearing his ~~brother~~ *brother's* tie. And ~~this~~ *that* isn't Mark's sports jacket either.
5. **A:** Those earrings look really good on Judy.
   B: Yeah. I like ~~these~~ *those* earrings too.

EXERCISE 7

Answers will vary.

UNIT 19 (pages 100–105)

EXERCISE 1

2. cup
3. That's
4. any
5. coffee
6. what
7. breakfast
8. I'm
9. some
10. banana
11. an
12. of

EXERCISE 2

2. l	6. a	10. e
3. c	7. k	11. g
4. f	8. i	12. d
5. j	9. b	

EXERCISE 3

2. a	9. some	15. an	20. a
3. some	10. a	16. some	21. some
4. some	11. some	17. some	22. some
5. some	12. some	18. a	23. some
6. a	13. some	19. some	24. some
7. some	14. an	OR a	OR a
8. an			

EXERCISE 4

2. any	5. some	7. some
3. any	6. some	8. any
4. some		

EXERCISE 5

2. bowl
3. a bottle of
4. cup
5. a glass of

EXERCISE 6

2. Fruit is good for you.
3. Are there any eggs for breakfast?
4. The candy is delicious.
5. Is the food at that restaurant good?
6. There is some bread.
7. Is there any milk?
8. These olives are salty.

EXERCISE 7

3. any	7. any	10. some
4. a	8. an	11. any
5. an	9. a	12. some
6. some		

EXERCISE 8

JUDY: Excuse me, waiter? Hi. Can I have ~~some~~ *a* glass of water, please?

WAITER: Sure, ma'am. Do you want mineral or regular?

JUDY: Regular, please.

[Minutes later]

WAITER: Here is your water. Are you ready to order?

JUDY: Yes. I'd like *a* sandwich and a bowl of soup. Oh, and ~~some~~ *a* small piece of chocolate cake too.

WAITER: And you, sir?

JOSH: Well, I'm not sure. ~~Are~~ *Is* the chicken here good?

WAITER: Yes, it's delicious.

JOSH: OK. I'd like ~~any~~ *some / Ø* chicken. And *a* bowl of ice cream.

WAITER: And what about something to drink?

JOSH: I want ~~the~~ _some_ water. Mineral water, please.

EXERCISE 9

Answers will vary.

UNIT 20 (pages 106–111)

EXERCISE 1

2. an
3. sale
4. size
5. any
6. the
7. on
8. fit
9. it
10. one
11. formal
12. ones

EXERCISE 2

2. don't fit
3. usually wear
4. often wear
5. Yellow
6. are
7. usually
8. _Answer will vary._

EXERCISE 3

2. e
3. b
4. c
5. d
6. a

EXERCISE 4

Answers will vary.
2. formal ones OR casual ones
3. expensive ones OR cheap ones
4. big one OR small one
5. bright one OR dull one

EXERCISE 5

2. a
3. a
4. the
5. a
6. the
7. The
8. a
9. the
10. the
11. an

EXERCISE 6

3. Ø
4. Ø
5. Ø
6. The
7. Ø
8. The
9. a
10. a
11. a
12. an

EXERCISE 7

2. A: Do you like the brown hat?

    B: No. I like the blue _one_.

3. A: Do you wear your ^black slacks to school?

    B: No, I usually wear my gray ~~one~~ _ones_.

4. A: Do you wear ~~the~~ _a_ tie to work?

    B: No, I don't like ~~the~~ ties.

5. A: Do you have ~~an~~ _a_ white dress that I could try on?

    B: Yes, I do. Here's a small one and here's a large one.

6. A: Do you want ~~a~~ _an_ umbrella?

    B: No, I never use ~~the~~ umbrellas.

EXERCISE 8

Answers will vary.

UNIT 21 (pages 112–118)

EXERCISE 1

2. can
3. pronunciation
4. can't do
5. Spanish
6. read
7. Can anyone
8. an idea
9. team
10. can't
11. teach
12. plan

EXERCISE 2

2. star
3. pass
4. fluent
5. team
6. ideas

EXERCISE 3

2. can't
3. can't
4. can
5. can
6. can't
7. can't
8. can

EXERCISE 4

Answers will vary.

EXERCISE 5

2. Can you give Kathy this message, please?
3. Can you tell me the answers, please?
4. Can you call the babysitter, please?
5. Can you wait for me, please?
6. Can you help me with my homework, please?

EXERCISE 6

3. can't dance / can play chess
4. can't sing / can't play the guitar
5. can play tennis / can cook well
6. can swim / can't play tennis
7. can't cook well / can't play chess
8. can play the guitar / can't be a coach
9. _Answers will vary._
10. _Answers will vary._

EXERCISE 7

2. **A:** Can you speak French?
   B: No, I can't.
3. **A:** Can Mike play the piano?
   B: No, he can't.
4. **A:** Can Rosie understand Italian?
   B: No, she can't.
5. **A:** Can the doctor see me tomorrow?
   B: Yes, he can. OR Yes, she can.
6. **A:** Can you go shopping with me today?
   B: No, I can't.

EXERCISE 8

Answers to questions will vary.

2. How can I learn your language?   Study it.
3. Who can cut my hair?   A hairstylist can.
4. Where can I buy CDs?   At the music store.
5. What can I do on the weekend in your town?   You can go dancing.

EXERCISE 9

       Can you
A: I have a problem. ~~You can~~ help me?
B: Sure. How ~~do~~ can I help?
A: I can't ~~not~~ understand the homework. Can you understand it?
    can   *Can*
B: Yes, I ~~do~~. But I can't ~~do~~ explain it well. ~~Cans~~ the teacher explain it to you?
A: I can't ~~do~~ find him.
                      help
B: He's in his office. I'm sure he can ~~helps~~ you.

EXERCISE 10

Answers will vary.

UNIT 22 (pages 119–123)

EXERCISE 1

2. missed
3. looked
4. convention
5. arrived
6. didn't finish
7. ended
8. checked out
9. I'm staying
10. apartment
11. party
12. Who's

EXERCISE 2

Answers will vary.

EXERCISE 3

2. watched
3. listened
4. checked in
5. visited
6. played

EXERCISE 4

3. arrived
4. didn't cook
5. enjoyed
6. studied
7. called
8. asked
9. didn't want
10. didn't buy

EXERCISE 5

2. ago
3. yesterday
4. last
5. ago
6. yesterday
7. last
8. yesterday
9. ago
10. last

EXERCISE 6

2. didn't watch
3. didn't talk
4. didn't enjoy
5. didn't play
6. didn't learn

EXERCISE 7

                             enjoyed
Thanks for dinner last week. I ~~enjoy~~ it very
             didn't
much. I hope I ~~not~~ talk too much. I ~~was~~ liked
                 showed
your kids a lot. Jeremy ~~did show~~ me some great computer games. I talked to Rita's secretary again
                     return
yesterday, but Rita didn't ~~returned~~ my call. Herb
               thank
P.S. Sorry I didn't ~~thanked~~ you before, but I was very busy.

EXERCISE 8

Answers will vary.

UNIT 23 (pages 124–128)

EXERCISE 1

2. actor
3. was born
4. began
5. acted
6. moved
7. made
8. happened
9. was
10. didn't have
11. Did
12. I did

EXERCISE 2

Base Form of Verb	Regular Verb	Irregular Verb
3. be born		✔
4. act	✔	
5. move	✔	
6. give up		✔
7. write		✔
8. become		✔
9. give		✔
10. fall		✔
11. injure	✔	
12. die	✔	

EXERCISE 3

2. took OR didn't take
3. slept OR didn't sleep
4. came OR didn't come
5. got OR didn't get
6. went OR didn't go
7. began OR didn't begin
8. fell OR didn't fall

EXERCISE 4

2. Sarah ate lunch today.
3. Matthew got up early today.
4. Yoshi slept eight hours last night.
5. Jay and Diego went to the library yesterday.
6. Jennifer Lopez made a movie last year.

EXERCISE 5

2. Henry didn't go to bed at 8:00.
3. Maria didn't eat breakfast at school.
4. John and Mary didn't make lunch at home.
5. Linda didn't see her friends at school.

EXERCISE 6

2. A: Did the teacher drink coffee in class last week?
   B: Yes, he did. OR Yes, she did.
3. A: Did you and your friends go to a party last week?
   B: No, we didn't.
4. A: Did Robert drink coffee today?
   B: No, he didn't.
5. A: Did Ann and Jeffrey fall off their bicycles today?
   B: Yes, they did.
6. A: Did your friends come to your home last week?
   B: No, they didn't.
7. A: Did your friends give you money today?
   B: Yes, they did.

EXERCISE 7

1. A: *Did you* ~~You did~~ sleep well last night?
   B: No, I ~~wasn't~~ *didn't*.
2. A: I ~~go~~ *went* to a party last Saturday.
   B: Did you have fun?
3. A: Did you eat anything last night?
   B: No, and I ~~not~~ *didn't* drink anything either.
4. A: I didn't ~~saw~~ *see* my keys on the table.
   B: We ~~gived~~ *gave* them to your roommate.
5. A: Did you ~~went~~ *go* to school yesterday?
   B: Yes, I went to school.

EXERCISE 8

Answers will vary.

UNIT 24 (pages 129–133)

EXERCISE 1

2. happen
3. did
4. happened
5. accident
6. didn't want
7. took
8. What
9. How
10. was
11. car
12. do

EXERCISE 2

2. f
3. a
4. e
5. b
6. d

EXERCISE 3

2. a
3. e
4. f
5. c
6. b

EXERCISE 4

2. Where
3. Who
4. What time
5. Why
6. What

EXERCISE 5

Answers will vary. Possible answers include:

2. When
3. What
4. Who
5. Who
6. What
7. Who
8. What

EXERCISE 6

2. you weren't
3. did you go
4. We went
5. Did you stay
6. We spent
7. We drove
8. we got
9. did you do
10. we stayed
11. talked
12. did you talk
13. I learned
14. Mark did
15. Did you meet
16. they had
17. came
18. did you meet OR you met
19. Was it
20. I enjoyed

EXERCISE 7

2. **A:** Who ~~did fix~~ *fixed* the car?

   B: My grandfather ~~fix~~ *fixed* it yesterday.

3. **A:** Why did you ~~took~~ *take* your car to the auto repair shop?

   B: Because a truck ~~hitted~~ *hit* my car and I had a big dent in the bumper.

4. **A:** Why ~~did your mother angry was~~ *was your mother angry* with you?

   B: I ~~drive~~ *drove* her car without her OK.

5. **A:** What time *did* the accident ~~happened~~ *happen*?

   B: It happened at 2:30.

6. **A:** How ~~the roads were~~ *were the roads*?

   B: They were slippery.

EXERCISE 8

Answers will vary.

UNIT 25 (pages 134–139)

EXERCISE 1

2. him
3. flowers
4. to
5. He
6. her
7. your
8. them
9. I
10. us
11. me
12. you

EXERCISE 2

Answers for names will vary.

2. b
3. f
4. a
5. h
6. j
7. i
8. e
9. d
10. c

EXERCISE 3

B: Hmm. What does she like?
A: Well, she likes sports.
B: How about a tennis racquet?
A: They are too expensive.
B: Then why don't you get her a gift certificate?
A: That's a good idea. I'll get her a gift certificate at a sporting goods store! Thanks!
B: Happy to help you.

EXERCISE 4

2. He needs a gift idea.
3. We want to go to the party.
4. It is not an appropriate gift.
5. He likes nuts and chocolate.
6. She didn't go to the party.

EXERCISE 5

2. Kathy drove it to the party.
3. I talked to them.
4. I didn't see you.
5. Bill loves it.
6. Bill talked to us.

EXERCISE 6

2. him
3. you / me
4. you OR it / it
5. it
6. her
7. them
8. us

EXERCISE 7

2. them / they / She
3. him / he
4. it / me
5. it / It
6. you / you / he
7. her / she
8. us / them

EXERCISE 8

Thank you for inviting ~~we~~ *us* to the party. The children and ~~me~~ *I* had a great time. The games were great. The kids loved ~~they~~ *them*.

Did Bob and Sally find the gifts? I left ~~it~~ *them* in their rooms. Did Bob like the tennis racquet? I bought it at Central Sports for ~~he~~ *him*. I got Sally's soccer ball there too. Does ~~her~~ *she* still play soccer? (I know you said "No gifts," but what's a birthday without gifts?)

Why don't ~~us~~ *we* meet one day for lunch? Give ~~I~~ *me* a call.

EXERCISE 9

Answers will vary.

EXERCISE 1

2. How many
3. were
4. That
5. time
6. much
7. was
8. hundreds
9. ate
10. people
11. did
12. expensive

EXERCISE 2

2. capital
3. flight
4. islands
5. plants
6. only

EXERCISE 3

Answers will vary. Possible answers include:
2. A lot. OR Not much.
3. None. OR Not many. OR A lot.
4. A lot. OR Not many. OR None.
5. A lot. OR Not many.
6. A lot. OR Not much. OR None.
7. A lot. OR Not many. OR None.
8. A lot. OR Not much.
9. A lot. OR Not many. OR None.
10. A lot. OR Not much.

EXERCISE 4

B: It was OK.
A: How much did you eat?
B: Just a little, because the food wasn't great. But the prices were good.
A: Really? How much did you spend?
B: Not much—only $30 for all of us.
A: How many people were there?
B: Four of us.

EXERCISE 5

2. c
3. b
4. c
5. c
6. b
7. a
8. c

EXERCISE 6

2.	How many oranges does Steve have?	Not many.
3.	How many bananas does Steve have?	Not many.
4.	How much milk does Steve have?	A lot.
5.	How many apples does Steve have?	A lot.
6.	How much soda does Steve have?	Not much.
7.	How much yogurt does Steve have?	Not much.
8.	How much juice does Steve have?	A lot.
9.	How many eggs does Steve have?	Not many.
10.	How much food does Steve have?	Not much.

EXERCISE 7

A: How ~~many~~ *much* time do you get for vacation?
B: Four weeks.

A: Do you spend *a* lot of time at home during your vacation?
B: No, only a ~~little~~ *few* days.
A: Where do you usually go?
B: We spend a ~~few~~ *little* time at my wife's parents' home. Then we go to the beach. We spend some time with our friends there.
A: How many ~~friend~~ *friends* do you see at the beach?
B: Not ~~much~~ *many*. Four or five.

EXERCISE 8

Answers will vary.

EXERCISE 1

2. went
3. is
4. are
5. they
6. It
7. is there
8. a
9. it's
10. there
11. a lot of
12. there's

EXERCISE 2

Answers will vary.

EXERCISE 3

3. are	**7.** aren't	**11.** isn't
4. aren't	**8.** are	**12.** 's
5. 's	**9.** 's	
6. is OR 's	**10.** are	

EXERCISE 4

Answers will vary. Possible answers include:

3. There is a drugstore in my neighborhood. OR There isn't a drugstore in my neighborhood.

4. There is a post office in my neighborhood. OR There isn't a post office in my neighborhood.

5. There is a library in my neighborhood. OR There isn't a library in my neighborhood.

6. There are a lot of stores in my neighborhood. OR There aren't many stores in my neighborhood.

7. There is a park in my neighborhood. OR There isn't a park in my neighborhood.

8. There is a bank in my neighborhood. OR There isn't a bank in my neighborhood.

9. There are some movie theaters in my neighborhood. OR There aren't any movie theaters in my neighborhood.

10. There are a lot of restaurants in my neighborhood. OR There aren't many restaurants in my neighborhood.

EXERCISE 5

2. Are there any banks on this block?

3. Is there a drugstore near here?

4. Are there any theaters in this area?

5. How many monuments are there in this area?

6. Is there an elevator in the mall?

7. Are there any good restaurants in the national park?

8. Is there an amusement park around here?

EXERCISE 6

2. there are	**8.** there isn't	
3. Are there	**9.** Is there	
4. there aren't	**10.** there is	
5. Is there	**11.** Is there	
6. there is	**12.** There is	
7. Is there		

EXERCISE 7

Greetings from Prague! We are having a great time here. Our hotel is very nice; ~~there's~~ *it's* a comfortable, reasonable place. It's close to everything we want to see.

There~~'s~~ *are* many things to see and do here. ~~They~~ *There* is a fantastic museum not very far from our room. We went to Old Town today. ~~It's~~ *There's* an unusual clock there.

It is so interesting! ~~They~~ *There* are also some beautiful statues there.

Let's see . . . ~~are~~ *is* there anything else? Oh, yes! We saw a very beautiful, old bridge yesterday. On the other side, ~~it~~ *there* was a castle! It's so amazing to be here. This place has a long, rich history.

I have to go now. We're going to see a movie tonight. Say hi to everyone for me.

EXERCISE 8

Answers will vary.

UNIT 28 (pages 152–156)

EXERCISE 1

2. a	**8.** modern	
3. old	**9.** major	
4. woman	**10.** fast	
5. chemistry	**11.** spy	
6. walks	**12.** similar	
7. an		

EXERCISE 2

2. honest man	**5.** computer science major	
3. personal ads	**6.** fun-loving man	
4. artistic woman	**7.** spy movies	

EXERCISE 3

Answers will vary.

EXERCISE 4

2. Venus and Serena Williams are famous athletes.

3. Jessica and Tim live in a big house.

4. Josh and Amanda ate at an awful restaurant.

5. Judy likes sad movies.

6. Buy this cool smart phone.

7. Jeremy bought an expensive flat-screen TV.

8. Bill and Mark have important jobs.

EXERCISE 5

2. They are interesting men.

3. The black dogs are friendly.

4. The expensive cars are over there.

5. The artistic students are young Italians.

6. The boring books have red covers.

7. The middle-aged actors are from China.

EXERCISE 6

Sentences may vary. Possible sentences include:

2. Beijing and Mexico City are big cities.
3. Ferraris and BMWs are expensive cars.
4. Prince Harry and Prince William are young men.
5. Quebec is a beautiful place.
6. Sushi is a Japanese food.
7. The Beatles were British singers.
8. The Bible is an old book.
9. Van Gogh was a poor artist.

EXERCISE 7

A: Where were you last night?
B: I had a date.
A: Really?
B: Yeah. I met ^a beautiful woman through a personal ad.
A: Oh, yeah? Tell me about her. Is she ~~so~~ active like you?
B: Yeah. She plays three ~~differents~~ *different* sports.
A: What else?
B: Well, she's a ~~person~~ very funny , *person* and she listens to ~~olds~~ *old* songs like I do.
A: Does she work?
B: Yeah. She has ~~a~~ *an* interesting job with a music company.
A: She sounds like she's the woman ~~perfect~~ *perfect* for you.
B: She is.

EXERCISE 8

Answers will vary.

UNIT 29 (pages 157–161)

EXERCISE 1

2. worse
3. better
4. older
5. snack
6. than
7. cheaper
8. beverages
9. entertainment
10. them
11. more
12. funny

EXERCISE 2

Answers will vary.

EXERCISE 3

One syllable: cold, dark, old, short, warm
Two syllables, ending in -y: busy, friendly, funny, healthy

Two syllables, not ending in -y: boring, honest
More than two syllables: artistic, difficult, exciting, expensive, important, interesting

EXERCISE 4

2. funnier
3. quicker
4. worse
5. more famous
6. better
7. more important
8. more expensive
9. heavier
10. cheaper

EXERCISE 5

2. busier
3. more difficult
4. shorter
5. funnier
6. better
7. more boring
8. more active
9. worse
10. colder

EXERCISE 6

2. more important than
3. quicker than
4. older than
5. warmer than
6. more crowded than
7. smaller than
8. worse than
9. cheaper than
10. friendlier than

EXERCISE 7

Answers may vary. Possible answers include:

2. Which is easier, swimming or water skiing?   (Answers will vary.)
3. Which are faster, planes or trains?   Planes.
4. Which is warmer, India or Russia?   India.
5. Which is more popular around the world, soccer or baseball?   Soccer.
6. Which is healthier, candy or fruit?   Fruit.

EXERCISE 8

A: So how's your new apartment? Is it ~~more good~~ *better* than your old one?
B: Yes, it is. It's larger and ~~more cheap~~ *cheaper*.
A: And where is it? Is the location good?
B: Oh, yeah. It's near the train station, so it's ~~more easy~~ *easier* for me to get to work. And I like the neighborhood too. It has a lot of trees and is ~~beautifuler~~ *more beautiful*. It's also ~~more~~ cleaner.

A: How many bedrooms are there in your apartment?

B: Well, there are three bedrooms. One bedroom is smaller ~~from~~ *than* the other two. It's ~~noisyer~~ *noisier* too. But the rest of the apartment is perfect. Why don't you come and see it this weekend?

A: That sounds like a good idea.

EXERCISE 9

Answers will vary.

UNIT 30 (pages 162–167)

EXERCISE 1

2. in
3. barbecue
4. Saturday
5. afternoon
6. free
7. on
8. two-story
9. at
10. volleyball
11. looking
12. 1:00

EXERCISE 2

2. are free
3. are looking forward to
4. have a barbecue
5. go shopping
6. play volleyball
7. go to a play
8. a two-story house

EXERCISE 3

2. at
3. on
4. on
5. in
6. in
7. in
8. on
9. in
10. in
11. at
12. at
13. on
14. at
15. on
16. at

EXERCISE 4

2. on
3. on
4. on
5. on
6. on
7. on
8. at
9. in
10. at
11. in
12. at
13. at
14. at

EXERCISE 5

Answers will vary. Possible answers include:

2. on Tuesdays and Fridays
3. on the weekends
4. on Thursday, the 3rd
5. on the 25th
6. on / November 17th
7. in
8. at / in / on
9. in the evening
10. on Friday, the 18th

EXERCISE 6

Answers will vary. Possible answers include:

2. I go to bed at 11:00 (at night).
3. I was born in 1985.
4. I was born in June.
5. My birthday is on May 15th.
6. They got married on May 18, 1980.
7. It starts at 9:00 and ends at 11:00.
8. I have English class on Mondays, Wednesdays, and Fridays.
9. I'm usually free at seven o'clock.
10. I usually spend time with my family on weekends.

EXERCISE 7

2. **A:** Is your birthday ~~on~~ *in* May?
   B: Yes, it is. It's on May 20th.
3. **A:** Do you ever work at ~~the~~ night?
   B: Sometimes. But I usually work in *the* morning.
4. **A:** When is your barbecue?
   B: It's ~~in~~ *at* 5:00 ~~at~~ *in* the evening.
5. **A:** What do you do ~~in~~ *on* weekends?
   B: ~~In~~ *On* Saturdays I go shopping.

EXERCISE 8

Answers will vary.

UNIT 31 (pages 168–173)

EXERCISE 1

2. game
3. little
4. going
5. player
6. not
7. soccer
8. football
9. sport
10. it's
11. start
12. to

EXERCISE 2

Team sport: baseball, basketball, football, hockey, soccer

Not a team sport: gymnastics, running, skiing, swimming

EXERCISE 3

2. b
3. a
4. b
5. a
6. b

EXERCISE 4

2. [They're] going to see a movie.
3. [He's] going to sleep.
4. [They're] going to have lunch.
5. [He's] going to buy some food.
6. [She's] going to go skiing.
7. [He's] going to exercise.
8. [They're] going to have a party.

EXERCISE 5

2. isn't going to spend OR 's not going to spend
3. aren't going to watch
4. isn't going to play OR 's not going to play
5. aren't going to visit
6. isn't going to take OR 's not going to take

EXERCISE 6

2. I'm going to eat out. OR I'm not going to eat out.
3. I'm going to go out with friends. OR I'm not going to go out with friends.
4. I'm going to go shopping. OR I'm not going to go shopping.
5. I'm going to go to a play. OR I'm not going to go to a play.
6. I'm going to play baseball. OR I'm not going to play baseball.
7. I'm going to have a barbecue. OR I'm not going to have a barbecue.
8. I'm going to visit relatives. OR I'm not going to visit relatives.
9. I'm going to wake up early. OR I'm not going to wake up early.
10. I'm going to work. OR I'm not going to work.

EXERCISE 7

I can't believe the course is almost over. ~~It~~ *It's*

going to end in one week. Most of my classmates
to
are going ˄ return home, but some are ~~no~~ *not* going to
is
leave. Rana ˄ going to start a new job. Misha is
take
going to ~~taking~~ another course. Masao and Laura
are
~~is~~ going to get married, and I'm going to go to their

wedding.

EXERCISE 8

Answers will vary.

EXERCISE 1

2. producer	8. to travel
3. news	9. Who's
4. It's	10. going
5. Are	11. I'm
6. be	12. isn't
7. are you	

EXERCISE 2

2. a	4. a	6. b	8. b
3. b	5. b	7. b	

EXERCISE 3

2. f	4. a	6. c	8. d
3. h	5. g	7. b	

EXERCISE 4

2. **A:** Is Laura Olson going to get a big part in the play?
   B: Yes, she is.
3. **A:** Are you and your classmates going to study tomorrow?
   B: No, we aren't. OR No, we're not.
4. **A:** Are Josh's parents going to move next year?
   B: Yes, they are.
5. **A:** Is Tim going to get a haircut?
   B: Yes, he is.
6. **A:** Are you going to stay in bed today?
   B: No, I'm not.

EXERCISE 5

2. Who is going to get a ticket?
3. Who is going to take something from the old woman?
4. What is the man in the black shirt going to take?
5. How is the old woman going to feel?
6. Where is the owner of the car going to go?
7. Why are the people going to go into the movie theater?
8. When is the movie going to start?

a. The owner of the car.
e. The man in the black shirt.
h. The woman's wallet.
g. Angry.
c. On a ski vacation.
d. Because they're going to see a movie.
b. At 5:00.

EXERCISE 6

2. When is it going to start?
3. What are you going to buy?
4. How are you going to get there?
5. Where is she going to go?
6. Who is going to clean it?

EXERCISE 7

Answers will vary.

EXERCISE 8

A: Did you hear the news? Amanda's pregnant.

B: That's awesome. When ~~she is~~ *is she* going to have the baby?

A: At the end of January. She's going to ~~stopping work~~ *stop working* in the middle of December.

B: Are we going *to* have a party for her?

A: Yes. We *are* going to have it in early December.

B: Wow, Amanda and her husband are *going* to have a baby!

A: ~~It~~ *It's* going to be very exciting for them.

B: What ~~is~~ *are* she and Josh going to name the baby?

A: I have no idea.

B: Where *are* they going to live? ~~They are~~ *Are they* going to move?

A: I think so. Their apartment is very small.

EXERCISE 9

Answers will vary.